PELICAN BOOKS

A288

INTRODUCTION TO
TYPOGRAPHY

OLIVER SIMON

INTRODUCTION

TO

TYPOGRAPHY

BY

OLIVER SIMON

'In order to succeed in an art, one must cultivate it throughout the whole of one's life.'—VOLTAIRE

PENGUIN BOOKS
IN ASSOCIATION WITH
FABER AND FABER

First Published in 1945
Second impression March 1946
Third impression 1947
Fourth impression 1949
Fifth impression (revised) 1953
Revised edition for Pelican Books 1954

Made and printed in Great Britain
for Penguin Books Ltd
Harmondsworth, Middlesex
at The Curwen Press Ltd

CONTENTS

INTRODUCTION

PRINTING is a way of life. It can transcend the boundaries of a trade and can take its place as one of the arts when the presiding genius at the printing office combines within himself the roles of business man, scholar, and artist. If he lacks business acumen and knowledge of the mechanics of the craft, the printing office must inevitably languish and finally cease to function. If he has not acquired a sufficient degree of scholarship, he cannot successfully attempt to be a book printer in the fullest sense of the term. If he is not something of an artist, he cannot hope to evolve and maintain a typographic style. These three qualities are seldom combined in one person, but the printer who is endowed with them is eligible for his place in the history of printing.

The study of the history of printing is important, for it is the masterpieces of the past that point a way to the contribution we, of this generation, can make to typographic art and practice. The fame and achievements of Aldus, Simon de Colines, the Estiennes, Jean de Tournes, Vascosan, Plantin, Baskerville, Bodoni, the early Didots, Bulmer, and Bensley, and many others, remain with us as an inspiration and a stimulus. Their best works are not only an unfailing source of pleasure but, in their typographic style, an expression of the civilization to which they were themselves an indispensable contribution.

Book typography has enriched the European scene for some five hundred years and continues to do so in our own time. Millions of books have been printed since the invention of printing. Many of these, admittedly, have been the humdrum efforts of ordinary tradesmen bent on making a living, but some books have been conceived with something more than the mere minimum of competence needed for strictly utilitarian and trade purposes. They have disclosed themselves to us and won our hearts through the excellence of their typographic style. This minority has been with us since the invention of printing, and will always be with us in greater or lesser degree.

Over fifteen thousand books of various kinds are printed in Great Britain every year; they comprise Bibles, Art Books, Fiction, Children's Books, Biographies, Autobiographies, Poetry, Plays, Histories, Scientific and Technical Books, Political Books, Textbooks, and School Books, and many more, including a large production of reprints of the Classics. A casual visitor to a bookshop would observe that all the books to be seen followed, superficially at least, a more or less definite convention in sizes and typography, and that the printing was either good, bad, or indifferent. In our present period, for instance, it would be noted that most novels are large or small crown 8vo, most biographies and autobiographies demy 8vo, which are sizes governed by the demands of public libraries. There would, for the same reason, be a certain similarity in thickness and, although the lettering on binding cases might vary in style, nearly all these books would be cased in boards and only a small number in paper wrappers. Again, an overwhelming majority of the books set on the Monotype machine would appear to our observer to have a further element in common, since only the current Monotype book faces available to the printer would be seen.

These rough-and-ready conventions of each period are necessary both for the practical management of the printing, publishing, and bookselling trades and, not least, for the establishment of a high degree of easy legibility for the reader. The need of achieving such easy legibility is one of the main reasons why typographic changes are slow in coming about.

One striking change of our century has been the mechanization of type-setting. The Monotype Corporation, which makes the machines and matrices for mechanical type-setting for printers in this country, have, during the last thirty years, introduced fresh type faces suitable to their machines and agreeable to the readers of books.

Paper also is now almost entirely machine-made, with the consequent disappearance of the 'deckle edge', a change that makes for convenience as well as cleanliness.

The 'finish' of machine-made paper is relatively smooth, so that the practice of damping paper (when it was hand-made) preparatory to printing has ceased to be necessary. Excellent presswork can be achieved on good machine-made papers, an excellence no less desirable than although different from that achieved by presswork on damped hand-made paper.

Binding cases have become simple in design, largely through the comprehensive mechanization of the binding trade. The book-jacket has become a necessity and offers a rich field for decoration. It keeps the books themselves clean in transit from printer to reader and, appropriately designed, has proved to be a first-class salesman and a valuable means of propaganda both for the publisher and the author. There are many other changes; we have merely touched on a few in an attempt to indicate how change comes about partly from the *outside*—the printer following the needs of the reader as new habits and conditions appear.

The printer and publisher can initiate change from the *inside*, for the typographic medium is, by its very nature and through the large choice of type faces and materials, subtly flexible. The full practice of Typography is an unending process of learning and a challenge to individual skill, imagination, and common sense, but this need not imply exhibitionism; authentic printing has no need to proclaim itself. Authors, too, have been known for their influence on Typography, while the demands of a mass of typographically conscious readers exert their influence.

There are many excellent books on Type Design, as well as the History, the Mechanics, and the Technics of Printing, and we shall not bring coals to Newcastle by covering the ground again, except incidentally. It is our endeavour rather to describe as briefly as possible from our own experience some of the many typographic fundamentals of book production.   o. s.

I

FOUNDATIONS

EXAMINATION of a well-produced book will show that a successful combination of its main essentials of type face, composition, margins, paper, presswork, and binding forms an harmonious and legible whole. To achieve harmony and legibility is the main object of typography. This needs knowledge, skill, and discipline—knowledge of type and traditions of printing—skill to assemble and manipulate the raw materials of book production—discipline to choose imaginatively what is appropriate and consistent.

For the practice of typography we must have men and tools—in other words, a well-trained staff and a well-equipped printing office. It is more difficult to obtain the former than the latter. That is an old problem, and we are reminded of an advertisement inserted by John Bell in the issue of *The World* of 11 July 1787, which reads:

PRESSMEN FOR BOOK-WORK

Wanted, Four Complete Press-men, who can execute Book-work in the most perfect manner, and who can be warranted for their regularity and sobriety. They may depend on constant employment so long as they execute their business perfectly; they will be paid by the piece or by the week, as may be most conducive to their own interest, and the satisfaction of their employer.

Composition, Presswork, and Proof-reading should indeed be of the highest standard possible, nor is it sufficient to have only a knowledge of printing practice and history; we must go further and make ourselves acquainted with the conditions of business of those we work for, namely the publisher and bookseller, who in their turn must not neglect the habits and just requirements of the reader.

Each printing office will have its own House Rules, and these rules will no doubt vary in detail between one House and another. Indeed, this is as it should be; books are written in many varieties, and there are in consequence various solutions to some of the typographical problems that arise. We have in this book occasionally submitted our own predilections for practices that are by no means uniform throughout the printing trade, notably in the matter of quotation marks, in the use of which our two oldest University Presses are divided. It is not infrequent for a publisher[1] to have his own House Rules too, which the printer may in some cases be obliged to follow, even if they contradict some points in his own. A printer's House Rules are, however, effective on most occasions; indeed, if they are wisely drafted they are more often than not accepted with gratitude. Furthermore, there is no doubt that they make for cohesion amongst the staff both old and new, which in turn produces the rudiments of a recognizable printing style. With these few general observations in mind, we can first of all present in this book some simple rules of composition for printers. We shall then examine step by step some of the many problems likely to present themselves to the printer on receipt of an average manuscript.

---

[1] Penguin Books, for instance, are publishers who have their own House Rules which contain some deviations from practices observed in this book.

RULES OF COMPOSITION

SPELLING AND PUNCTUATION

THE carefully prepared MS. of a precise author must be strictly followed as to punctuation and spelling, so also must extracts quoted from other works. Many writers leave some of the details of punctuation of their copy to the printer. An intelligent interpretation of an author's meaning by means of correctly placed punctuation marks is an art that can be acquired only by long experience, and for which no hard-and-fast rules can be formulated. Many valuable hints on spelling, punctuation, italicizing, capitalization, divisions of words, and other matters of style, are to be found in the Oxford Rules,[1] which can be taken mostly as a standard authority. Collins's Dictionary[2] gives useful hints on the italicizing of foreign words, abbreviations, and unusual spellings, and contains much useful biographical and geographical information.

Titles, displayed lines, chapter heads, running headlines, page heads, dates, the names of speakers in plays (where these occupy a line to themselves), are not to be followed by a full point. But captions to blocks etc. should take a full point, except when they consist of one line only.

QUOTATION MARKS

Use single quotation marks (') outside and double (") only for quotations within quotations. If there should be another quotation within the second, use the single quotation marks. Where long extracts are indented or set in smaller type, quotation marks are not to be used. Punctuation marks used at the end of a quoted passage must be inside the quotation marks if they belong to the quotation,

---

[1] *Rules for Compositors and Readers at the University Press, Oxford.* 36th Edition. 1952.

[2] *Authors' and Printers' Dictionary*, by F. Howard Collins. 9th Edition, 15th Impression. 1953. Oxford University Press.

otherwise outside. When isolated words or an incomplete sentence are quoted the punctuation mark is placed outside the 'quotes', with the exception of the interrogation mark (?) and the exclamation (!), which are placed inside the 'quotes' if they belong to the quotation. When a quotation is complete, the 'quotes' are placed outside the full point.

PARENTHESES AND BRACKETS

Parentheses ( ) are used chiefly to denote interpolations, and brackets [ ] are used to show notes or explanations, or words assumed to be omitted from original MSS. and added by subsequent editors. They may also be used to indicate the correct spelling of a mis-spelt word.

Occasionally parentheses are needed within parentheses, and although it is sometimes recommended to use them thus (( )), it is our opinion that the subsidiary interpolation is more clearly shown by the use of brackets within the parentheses thus ([ ]). Where the bracket and parenthesis fall together at the end, a thin space should be inserted between them.

CAPITALIZATION

No definite rules can be laid down for the use of initial capitals. When rightly used they give emphasis to important words to which the author wishes to give prominence, and the carefully prepared MS. of the writer who knows what he wants must be strictly followed. Here are a few of the more familiar words where the initial capital is usual:

His Majesty, Dark Ages, London Clay, Bagshot Beds, Upper Greensand (in geology), Lady Day, Berkeley Square.

Denominational terms and names of parties, as Baptist, Presbyterian, Liberal, Conservative, Socialist, Fascist.

Nature, Time, Death, and other abstract nouns when personified, e.g.: O Death, where is thy sting?

When a person is addressed by his rank instead of by name, an initial capital letter is used, e.g.:

'Good morning, Colonel.'

'Oh, Father, how delightful it is to be home again! How is Mother, and where is she?' *but* 'Your mother (l.c.) is in the garden, little dreaming of the surprise awaiting her.'

Capitalize pronouns and synonyms referring to the Deity: Almighty, Christ, Father, God, He, Himself, His, Jehovah, Lord, Me, Mine, Thee, the Holy Trinity, Thine, Thy; *but* who, whom, whose (l.c.).

Figure, Number, Plate (Fig., No., Pl.) should each begin with a capital letter.

Do not use capital S or E, etc., in such expressions as southern Italy, eastern Europe. But names of *political divisions* such as Southern Rhodesia, Northern Ireland, Western Australia, should have initial capitals.

SMALL CAPITALS

Small capitals are used for the purpose of giving more emphasis to a word or sentence than can be conveyed by printing the same in italic. They may also be employed for chapter headings and head-lines, and for various purposes of display in the preliminaries of a book. Small capitals should be letter-spaced.

ITALIC

Italic is used for emphasis and for the names of books, magazines, newspapers, films, plays, and operas, appearing in the text; also for foreign words and phrases; but extracts from foreign texts, however short, should be in roman. The title of an article from a magazine should be in roman, 'quoted', and the name of the magazine itself in italic. Similarly, individual poems quoted from a volume of poetry should be in roman, 'quoted', while the title of the volume itself should be in italic. Names of pictures should be in roman, 'quoted'. Names of ships to be in italic; prefixes and the possessive 's' to be in roman, e.g.: The *Aquitania*'s hull.

In music, song titles are to be roman, 'quoted', and subject-titles to be italic as, for example, Verdi's *Falstaff*, Bizet's *Carmen*, *but* Bach's Mass in B minor, 'Waldstein' Sonata, Beethoven's Fifth Symphony.

Musical terms of expression should be in roman, but in italics for their contracted form: forte, piano, but *f*, *p*, *pp*, *mf*, etc.

DIVISION OF WORDS

Close spacing involves more frequent division of words, but the following rules should be applied as far as possible. Divide after a vowel, turning over the consonant. In present participles take over -ing, as divid-ing, rest-ing. When two consonants come together put the hyphen between them, as haemor-rhage, forget-ting, trick-ling. The terminations -tion, -cious, -cial may be taken over entire, but must not themselves be divided. The part of the word at the end of a line should suggest the remainder of the word: starva-tion, *not* star-vation. A broken word should not be allowed to end a page, neither should it end the last full line of a paragraph if it is at all possible to avoid it.

Words derived from Latin and Greek should be divided so that each component part retains its complete form. For example: philo-sophy, archaeo-logy, geo-graphy, manu-script, litho-graphy, laryngo-logy, atmo-sphere.

FIGURES

In descriptive matter numbers under 100 should be in words, but figures should be used when the matter consists of a sequence of stated quantities, numbers, ages, etc. Spell out indefinite numbers, e.g. 'has been done a thousand times'. Insert commas with four or more figures, 2,391. To represent an approximate date use the fewest figures possible, 1931–2, *not* 1931–32, and divide the figures by an en rule, *not* a hyphen. Dates should be set as written in descriptive matter, i.e. 'on the 20th of January 1931', but for the headings of letters, and wherever possible, set 20 January 1931. Set 250 B.C. *but* A.D. 250. In B.C. references always put the full date in a group of years, 185–122 B.C.

SETTING

Spacing should be as even as possible. Lower-case matter should be set with a thin or middle space between words rather than a thick or wider. It is not necessary to increase the space after a full stop or after ? ! ; : ' . A hair space should be inserted before the apostrophe in such phrases as that's (that is), colonel's (colonel is), in order to distinguish from the possessive case. A hair space should precede ; : ? ! and should be inserted between the opening quote and the first word. The first line of a paragraph should not be indented more than one em. Small capitals should be letter-spaced. Capital letters also should be letter-spaced when possible. All roman numerals set in capitals or small capitals should be hair-spaced. When blocks of capitals are used, the space between letters and words should be distinctly less than between lines. Avoid using short rules to divide display lines and paragraphs.

VOWEL-LIGATURES

The combinations *ae* and *oe* should each be printed as two letters in Latin, Greek, and English words: Aetna, Boeotia, larvae.

The ligatures *æ* and *œ* should, however, be used in Old English and French words: Ælfric, Cædmon, manœuvre, hors d'œuvre.

REFERENCES TO AUTHORITIES

Citation of authorities at the end of quotations should be printed as:

HERODOTUS, *Histories*, vi. 129

and at heads of chapters should usually be in contracted form:

HOR. *Epis*. i. ii. 12   VIRG. *Eclog*. i. 6-7

Frequent citations in notes usually have the author's name in lower case, as:

Gibbon's *Decline and Fall*, vol. iii, p. 25

References to the Bible: 2 Samuel xvii. 25

References to Shakespeare's plays: *2 Henry IV*, II. i. 55

FOLIOS

Folios should be in the same size type as text and in lower-case roman numerals, starting from the half-title and recommencing in arabic figures from folio one at the first page of text or half-title of text, if any.

CONTENTS

The Contents should be a list of the constituent chapters of the body. The type of the Contents page must conform in face to that of the body of the book, and the heading must conform to that of the chapter.

MAKE-UP

Books should normally be made up in the following order:

Half-title	Preface
Title	Introduction
'History'[1] of book, with imprint	Corrigenda or errata (if any)[2] Text of book
Dedication	Appendix
Acknowledgements	Author's Notes
Contents	Glossary
List of Illustrations	Bibliography
List of Abbreviations	Index

All the above, except the 'history' of the book, with the printer's imprint, begin generally on a right-hand page.

RUNNING HEAD-LINES

Running head-lines, when used, should begin on the second page of text, and unless instructions are given to

[1] Date of publication, and dates of subsequent reprints and revised editions.

[2] Where a single error is mentioned, 'Corrigendum' or 'Erratum' is correct.

the contrary should consist of the title of the book for left-hand pages, and the title of the chapter for the right-hand pages. Preliminary matter should be headed 'Contents', 'Introduction' etc. on both sides.

ILLUSTRATIONS

Full-page illustrations should, where possible, be printed on the right-hand side of the opening.

CAPTIONS

Captions to illustrations in the text should generally be set in type two points smaller than the main body of the work.

APPENDIX

The type of the heading of the Appendix must conform to that of the chapter head, but the text may be one or two points smaller than the text of the book. Where there is more than one Appendix or Index, the plural form Appendixes or Indexes should normally be used, the alternative Appendices and Indices being reserved for medical and scientific works.

INDEX

An Index of two or more columns is to be preferred, set in type two points smaller than the text of the book. Begin each letter of the alphabet with even small capitals if an initial is not specified. Print page numbers immediately after the last word, with a comma before the figures. Divide columns by a white space, not by a rule.

FOOTNOTES

Footnotes are to be indicated by superior figures, and should be two points smaller than the text type. They must be separated from the text by a white space, not by a rule. Notes to a short page must be brought down to the foot of the page and not 'skied'. If it is found necessary to break a footnote, the portion turned over takes precedence over other footnotes on that page.

MARKS USED IN THE CORRECTION OF PROOFS

L—— Every period of civilization which forms a complete and consistent whole, manifests itself not only in
political life, in religion, art and science, but also sets its
characteristic stamp on social life. Thus the Middle Ages
had their courtly and aristocratic manners and etiquette,
differing but little in the various countries of Europe; as
well as their peculiar forms of middle-class life. Italian
customs at the time of the Renaissance offer in these
respects the sharpest contrast Mediaevalism. The foundation on which they rest is wholly different. Social intercourse in its highest and most perfect form now ignored all
distinctions of caste, and was based simply on the existence
of an educated class as we now understand the word.
word. Birth and origin were without influence, unless
combined with leisure and inherited wealth. Yet this
assertion must not be taken in an absolute and unqualified sense, since mediaeval distinctions still sometimes

CORRECTED

EVERY period of civilization which forms a complete and
consistent whole, manifests itself not only in political life,
in religion, art and science, but also sets its characteristic
stamp on social life. Thus the Middle Ages had their
courtly and aristocratic manners and etiquette, differing
but little in the various countries of Europe, as well as their
peculiar forms of middle-class life.

Italian customs at the time of the Renaissance offer in
these respects the sharpest contrast to Mediaevalism. The
foundation on which they rest is wholly different. Social
intercourse in its highest and most perfect form now
ignored all distinctions of caste, and was based simply on
the existence of an educated class as we now understand
the word. Birth and origin were without influence, unless
combined with leisure and inherited wealth. Yet this assertion must not be taken in an absolute and unqualified
sense, since mediaeval distinctions still sometimes made

3

CHOOSING THE TYPE FACE

'TYPE, the voice of the printed page, can be legible and dull, or legible and fascinating, according to its design and treatment. In other words, what the booklover calls readability is not a synonym for what the optician calls legibility.'[1] There are, in fact, aesthetic considerations which prompt people to prefer one type rather than another, considerations closely linked with the emotions and difficult to define precisely. Likewise, aesthetics are a dominant factor for those who prefer a classic to be reprinted in a type indicative of its own 'period', and similar to this is the effort to produce 'atmosphere' aided by the choice of type face. Again, illustrated books raise their own aesthetic problems in the choice of a type. But to an equal degree it can be claimed that the choice of type face is dependent on such practical considerations as the kind of book, the particular public to which the book must appeal, its length, its size, the type area to be decided, the type size, and finally the leading. The paper to be used is always a factor to be taken into consideration. Owing to the great diversity of authors' MSS. it is obviously impossible to suggest a printer's reaction to every occasion, but, for our own purpose, we can examine the deservedly popular Monotype book faces in current use shown on pages 14 and 15, and try to ascertain the reasons why, under certain conditions, we would choose one type face rather than another.

Some, or all, of these type faces have had the support of our most eminent practitioners because of their high degree of legibility and the grace of their letter forms. They are, in their way, a cross-section of our typographical world, in that we have represented types revived from an earlier age, new types, and types which are a compromise between the old and the new. Figures 1 and 2 on pages 14

[1] Paul Beaujon: *The Monotype Recorder*, Vol. 32, No. 1. 1933.

and 15 show all the sizes in 12 pt., a size which, on the average, is the test of the norm of a book face. We are aware that a type viewed as a specimen may be one thing, whilst a type in use may somehow look different. How a type is *used* (measure, spacing, leading, paper on which it is printed, inking) is of primary importance. Leading, for instance, has the optical effect of altering the colour[1] values of the type on the printed page: the greater the amount of leading the lighter in colour a type appears. The colour value of type is also affected by the kind of paper on which type is printed. Again, some types such as Caslon, Garamond, and Perpetua attain their finest flowering in their larger sizes, whilst Fournier, Plantin, and Imprint are, for various reasons, more successful in their smaller sizes.

Our fifteen type faces shown on pages 14 and 15, when compared, show several important differences concerning:

    (*a*) Width of letters
    (*b*) Size of the type face on the type body
    (*c*) Shading of the thick strokes
    (*d*) Length of ascenders and descenders
    (*e*) Size of capital letters
    (*f*) General weight and colour of the type face.

These differences, as we shall see, have a practical importance of their own apart from any aesthetic considerations.

(*a*) WIDTH OF LETTERS

Although the type faces shown on pages 14 and 15 are all set in 12 pt., nevertheless the length of the alphabet varies in both capitals and lower-case. This variation affects the number of words that can conveniently be printed on a page, exclusive of any necessity, or otherwise, of leading. The roman lower-case letters of Scotch and Baskerville, for instance, are wide and generous, whilst, at the other extreme, Fournier and Bembo occupy considerably less width. This obvious difference in width of letters, or 'set'

[1] A black impression can range from jet black to grey; see page 17.

as it is called in the trade, will frequently be an important consideration in choosing a type for a short book on the one hand, or a very long book on the other, and types that are width-saving have obvious attractions for books set in double column. But this is, after all, only one of several considerations in choosing a type: there are other factors which we must examine and which, in their turn, contribute their influence to our choice.

(b) SIZE OF THE TYPE FACE ON THE TYPE BODY

A further examination of the types on pages 14 and 15 shows very considerable differences in the size of the actual type face on the 12-pt. body. These differences become even more obvious the larger the type sizes become. If a page of each of these fifteen type faces were set solid, the size of the actual face on the 12-pt. body would not affect the number of words per square inch except in so far as the 'set' of the face is wide or narrow. But the size of the type face on the body does give a pointer to the body size that might be chosen with a view to the maximum legibility in combination with the degree of leading compatible with an agreeable page of type. Plantin and Times, for instance, are, in relation to others, so large on their bodies that whilst 12 pt. is the norm for almost all the types exhibited, the equivalent could well be 11 pt. in their case (Fig. 4). This 'largeness' on the body is measured first in terms of the height of the non-ascending and non-descending lower-case letters, e.g. x (hence the term 'x-height'), and secondly, the width of the m (which determines the 'set'). A type like Times may thus be described as large on the body but of narrow set.

Types that are, or tend to be, large on their bodies benefit from being set leaded in all sizes except when the measure is narrow. This helps legibility and enhances any aesthetic appeal a type may possess, notably Times, Baskerville, Bodoni, Garamond, Imprint, Plantin, and Scotch.

TYPE FACES FOR
TEXT COMPOSITION

Showing Alphabet Widths

Scotch 46   abcdefghijklmnopqrstuvwxyz
abcdefghijklmnopqrstuvwxyz
ABCDEFGHIJKLMNOPQRSTUVWXYZ
ABCDEFGHIJKLMNOPQRSTUVWXYZ

Times 327   abcdefghijklmnopqrstuvwxyz
abcdefghijklmnopqrstuvwxyz
ABCDEFGHIJKLMNOPQRSTUVWXYZ
ABCDEFGHIJKLMNOPQRSTUVWXYZ

Baskerville 169 abcdefghijklmnopqrstuvwxyz
abcdefghijklmnopqrstuvwxyz
ABCDEFGHIJKLMNOPQRSTUVWXYZ
ABCDEFGHIJKLMNOPQRSTUVWXYZ

Bell 341   abcdefghijklmnopqrstuvwxyz
abcdefghijklmnopqrstuvwxyz
ABCDEFGHIJKLMNOPQRSTUVWXYZ
ABCDEFGHIJKLMNOPQRSTUVWXYZ

Imprint 101 abcdefghijklmnopqrstuvwxyz
abcdefghijklmnopqrstuvwxyz
ABCDEFGHIJKLMNOPQRSTUVWXYZ
ABCDEFGHIJKLMNOPQRSTUVWXYZ

Plantin 110 abcdefghijklmnopqrstuvwxyz
abcdefghijklmnopqrstuvwxyz
ABCDEFGHIJKLMNOPQRSTUVWXYZ
ABCDEFGHIJKLMNOPQRSTUVWXYZ

Bodoni 135   abcdefghijklmnopqrstuvwxyz
abcdefghijklmnopqrstuvwxyz
ABCDEFGHIJKLMNOPQRSTUVWXYZ
ABCDEFGHIJKLMNOPQRSTUVWXYZ

Figs. 1 and 2

Caslon 128   abcdefghijklmnopqrstuvwxyz
abcdefghijklmnopqrstuvwxyz
ABCDEFGHIJKLMNOPQRSTUVWXYZ
ABCDEFGHIJKLMNOPQRSTUVWXYZ

Garamond 156   abcdefghijklmnopqrstuvwxyz
abcdefghijklmnopqrstuvwxyz
ABCDEFGHIJKLMNOPQRSTUVWXYZ
ABCDEFGHIJKLMNOPQRSTUVWXYZ

Walbaum 374   abcdefghijklmnopqrstuvwxyz
abcdefghijklmnopqrstuvwxyz
ABCDEFGHIJKLMNOPQRSTUVWXYZ
ABCDEFGHIJKLMNOPQRSTUVWXYZ

Ehrhardt 453   abcdefghijklmnopqrstuvwxyz
abcdefghijklmnopqrstuvwxyz
ABCDEFGHIJKLMNOPQRSTUVWXYZ
ABCDEFGHIJKLMNOPQRSTUVWXYZ

Fournier 185   abcdefghijklmnopqrstuvwxyz
abcdefghijklmnopqrstuvwxyz
ABCDEFGHIJKLMNOPQRSTUVWXYZ
ABCDEFGHIJKLMNOPQRSTUVWXYZ

Bembo 270   abcdefghijklmnopqrstuvwxyz
abcdefghijklmnopqrstuvwxyz
ABCDEFGHIJKLMNOPQRSTUVWXYZ
ABCDEFGHIJKLMNOPQRSTUVWXYZ

Centaur 252   abcdefghijklmnopqrstuvwxyz
abcdefghijklmnopqrstuvwxyz
ABCDEFGHIJKLMNOPQRSTUVWXYZ
ABCDEFGHIJKLMNOPQRSTUVWXYZ

Perpetua 239   abcdefghijklmnopqrstuvwxyz
abcdefghijklmnopqrstuvwxyz
ABCDEFGHIJKLMNOPQRSTUVWXYZ
ABCDEFGHIJKLMNOPQRSTUVWXYZ

NOTE: These types are 12 pt. on a 12-pt. body, with the exception of Walbaum (reproduced from a type on a Continental body), which is Didot cast on a 13-pt. body; and Times, which is set with long descenders, requiring a 13 pt. body.

(*c*) SHADING OF THE THICK STROKES

One of the characteristics of a type face is the contrast of the thick and thin strokes; this has a practical significance. In those types where the contrast is most pronounced, the shading of the rounded strokes might be described as vertical, notably in Bodoni, Scotch, and Walbaum. We submit that types with heavy vertical shading should always be set leaded in all sizes, otherwise the lines, if set solid, would have a dazzling effect to the eyes. Baskerville stands midway between vertical and rounded shading and is enhanced by being set leaded. Bembo, Caslon, Garamond, Perpetua, and Centaur are examples of rounded and more gradual shading, and as Bembo, Caslon, and Centaur are, in addition, small faces on their bodies, leading is not so essential.

Walbaum
Vertical Shading

Perpetua
Rounded Shading

Fig. 3

(*d*) LENGTH OF ASCENDERS AND DESCENDERS

There are five letters in the lower-case alphabet with descenders, g, j, p, q and y, and six with ascenders, b, d, f, h, k and l. The ascending and descending letters give an automatic amount of apparent white spacing between the lines of type solidly set. When the ascenders and descenders are long, this white appears to be greater, but on the other hand, the face is, as a result, small on the body. Times normally has short ascenders and descenders but there is also available a version in which the ascenders and descenders are long. In this version the 12-pt. face is, out of necessity, on a 13-pt. body; 12 pt. Walbaum is also on a 13-pt. body. It was found expedient to put the 12 pt. Walbaum on a 13-pt. body to achieve a faithful reproduction of an old but still existing typefounders' type cast on a Didot (Continental) body. Other types, as may be seen on pages 14 and 15, have medium length ascenders and descenders, which show these types to appear large though remaining on a 12-pt. body.

(e) SIZE OF CAPITAL LETTERS

The capitals of most type faces are the height of the ascenders of their lower case, but in Bembo and Perpetua the capitals range lower, e.g., Thames (Bembo), Plaistow (Perpetua).

A type with capitals ranging lower than the lower-case ascenders is useful for books where there are more than the usual number of words capitalized in the text, or where whole words or even sentences occur frequently in the main text in capitals, or, again, if the book is a bibliography or a catalogue.

(f) GENERAL WEIGHT AND COLOUR OF THE TYPE FACE

Some readers have a preference for fully coloured types such as Plantin, Times, Bodoni, Scotch, and Ehrhardt, whilst others find types lighter or medium in colour easier to read, e.g., Fournier and Caslon. This is generally a matter of habit or eyesight, but there is little doubt, for instance, that children prefer a black-looking type. Leading or absence of leading, together with the choice of paper, will affect the colour of a type, making colourful type faces appear lighter than they normally are, and vice versa. We shall refer to these two factors in greater detail in a section to follow.

There are, to be sure, other and more mundane factors in choosing a type face. The number of type faces a printer can stock has its limits financially, nor at any given time are the type faces he possesses necessarily complete with accented letters, bolds, and old style and modern numerals. Nor will he always have a sufficient range of sizes of every type face in his stock. For certain books therefore which demand any or all of the above-mentioned special sorts, or an abnormal number of sizes of a fount, a printer will naturally be inclined to consider what he has conveniently to hand.

The conception of the Beautiful must, it is true, not be confounded with those of the Good and the Useful; none the less, the three are, in reality, but different aspects from varying angles of one and the same thing. The measure of the virtue in a printed book is the number of people who read it and the frequency, eagerness, and speed with which it is read: indeed, the oftener a book is read—assuming it to be good—the

12 pt. Plantin solid, type face full on the body

greater the pleasure and profit resulting to the mind. Moreover, this same adaptation to the standards required by our eyes, which discriminate between fount and fount, constitutes its beauty. This varies according as it succeeds in delighting them by sure proportionment of details, charm, and perfection, not only at a first glance but in the long run. It often happens that we have the same book before our eyes for a long time. If it turns out less and less agreeable to the

12 pt. Bembo solid, small on body, easier to read than above, owing to the white space between the lines given by the smallness of the type face on its body.

eye, so that it becomes wearisome more quickly than any other, our opinion of its merits will sink. Visual powers vary largely in different people; we must not, therefore, expect every pair of eyes to be equally attracted, or repelled, by the same type: and this is one of the principal reasons why books should by no means all be printed after the same fashion. Beauty in books may be classified under three different

11 on 12 pt. Baskerville, very full on body, the optical equivalent in size of 12 pt. Bembo above.

Fig. 4

POETRY IS INDEED

SOMETHING DIVINE. IT IS

at once the centre and circumference of knowledge; it is that which comprehends all science, and that to which all science must be referred ... It is the perfect and consummate surface and bloom of all things; it is as the odour and the colour of the rose to the texture of the elements which compose it, as the form and splendour of unfaded beauty

to the secrets of anatomy and corruption. What were virtue, love, patriotism, friendship—what were the scenery of this beautiful universe which we inhabit; what were our consolations on this side of the grave—and what were our aspirations beyond it, if poetry did not ascend to bring light and fire from those eternal regions where the owl-winged faculty of calcula-

FOR GENERATIONS

EVERY DIDOT WAS A MAN

of letters as well as a printer, for whom a book was something to be read and admired: more than merchandise on the one hand and more than an act of creation or a conjuring trick on the other. 'Un bon imprimeur doit faire la nuance entre l'homme de lettres et l'artiste,' said Pierre. The Didots did not regard themselves as magicians, but

as links in the production of something important. Firmin Didot thought in the terms of books, while Giambattista Bodoni thought in terms of print. Every Didot somehow left his mark on the world of letters. Old François, Firmin's father, was a fine classical scholar, and years after he was supposed to have retired he was busy in his son's office going

Fig. 5. (Above) Fournier: small on its body.
(Below) Ehrhardt: large on its body set in equivalent sizes as above.

4

SETTING OF THE TEXT

THE MANUSCRIPT

A PRINTER receives MSS. of endless variety and it would be impossible to suggest any one procedure to cover all occasions. A publisher of repute would, in all probability, have read carefully through the MS. before sending it to the printer. Nevertheless, as a precaution, the printer should immediately give it a cursory examination as to content. He must then assure himself, in certain categories of MS., that there is nothing which offends against either the law of libel or obscenity and, in time of war or civil commotion, that there is nothing contravening the regulations applying to censorship as imposed by the authorities.

The MS. should then be examined for punctuation and spelling, to see that the author has prepared it carefully and to note to what degree it conforms to the rule of the House. The spelling, punctuation, capitalization, etc., of an obviously careless author can well be improved by an experienced Press Reader, who should also be responsible for checking dates, titles, place-names, historical characters, etc. As De Vinne says: 'It is the belief now, as it was in the days of Moxon, the first English writer on the technics of printing, that it is the duty of the printer to supplement the negligences of the writer'.[1]

MARGINS

Margins set off and enhance the type area, just as the mount of a drawing displays a picture to its fullest advantage. Both margins and mounts are subject to the laws of proportion. The margins on the pages of a book help the

[1] *The Practice of Typography: Correct Composition*, by Theodore Low De Vinne. 1916.

eye to focus on the type area: indeed our eyes are accustomed to certain conventions, and any marked deviation means an interruption in the flow of the reading.

There should be more margin at the bottom of a page than at the top, otherwise the type area has the appearance of falling out of the page. The inner margins should be less than the outer margins, as a double text-page opening strikes the eye as an entity, not as two single pages separate in themselves. Enough room should be left on the side margins for easy manipulation of the reader's thumb or finger without obscuring type matter. The bottom margin should be large enough for the comfortable placing of the reader's thumb, particularly at the period when the last lines of the page are being read. Good margins are an aid to legibility (Figs. 6 and 7), and, apart from the above considerations, the larger amount of margin on sides, head, and tail allows for subsequent cutting and rebinding without injury to the type area. Ample margins also give room to the reader for annotation.

When a book is printed with hanging shoulder (marginal) notes to the text, they must be considered, typographically, as part of the type area of the text, and the surrounding margin should consequently make allowance for these notes (Fig. 8).

In pocket editions, where the text has to be condensed into a small area, margins are inevitably slight. The pages are therefore imposed a little above the optical centre of the page, whilst the merely nominal inner and side margins will be equal (Fig. 9).

When type face, type size and margins have been chosen provisionally, a cast-off can be made of the MS., which will be shown to make a book of x pages.

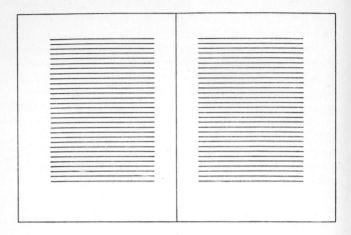

Fig. 6. Suggested margins for a quarto book

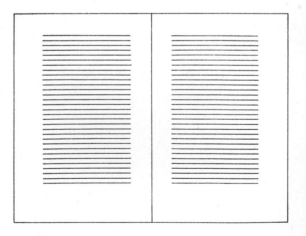

Fig. 7. Suggested margins for an octavo book

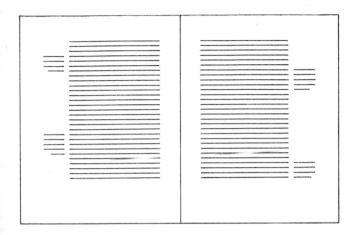

Fig. 8. Quarto book, showing margins allowing for hanging
shoulder notes.

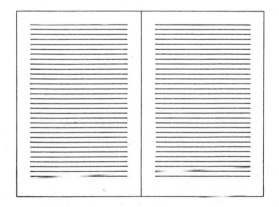

Fig. 9. Pocket edition, with slight margins

B

THE TEXT PAGE

The ordinary text page is the basic unit of a book, providing a foundation from which the typographic style of the pre-liminary pages evolves. There are many kinds of books and, within strict limits, many ways of setting them, but the pages of well-set books will all present to the eye and mind an inevitable sense of the suitability of composition to their content and purpose. This involves a high degree of judgement in the choice of type face, type size, type area, margins, leading; and in the treatment of head-lines, quoted matter, chapter openings, etc.

The size of the type and the width of the type measure should allow the eye to follow the line of type without strain (Figs. 4 and 5) and easily travel back to pick up the next line; in other words the page should be legible.[1]

The problem varies according to the kind of book: a novel or biography generally implies rapid reading throughout, whilst in poetry the tempo would be slower. Works of reference and dictionaries, on the other hand, are read only for specific entries. The leading of the page aids legibility, particularly when the type size is under 12 pt.

Types large in point size which are set to a narrow measure tend to produce an abnormal number of breaks in words at the ends of the lines of each page. This is not conducive to legibility, and offsets the benefits of a large type face, which may nevertheless be too large for the width of the type area.

The last word of the last line of a text page should not be broken, for it will then be possible for the reader to avoid the irritating necessity of having to pick up the concluding syllable of a word on the opposite or even a verso page.

[1] 'By legibility I mean a proper observance in all its infinite details of that principle of order and convention which is the basis of written communication. Printing is the vehicle: legibility is the well-greased bearing that allows the wheels of sense to revolve without squealing.'—Francis Meynell, *The Monotype Recorder*, Vol. 32, No. 3. 1933.

'You ask me where one can find happiness in this world. After many experiments, I have convinced myself that it rests entirely in feeling satisfied with oneself. The passions can never make us happy, we always want the impossible, and are never content with what we have. I suppose that some people, blessed with unfailingly virtuous natures, possess a good deal of the contentment that I think of as being a condition of happiness, but for myself, since I'm not good enough to be self-satisfied, I make up for it by the real satisfaction that work can give.

10 pt. Baskerville solid

Work does afford a genuine sense of well-being and increases one's indifference to pleasures that are pleasures in name only, the amusements that society people have to be content with. And there, my dear, you have my small philosophy, and it's a certainty, especially when I'm feeling well. At the same time, it should not prevent us from snatching such little diversions as may come our way from time to time; an occasional love-affair, a beautiful countryside, travel, such things leave enchanting memories, and you think of them when you are far

10 on 11 pt. Baskerville

away and can no longer enjoy them. They make a little store of happiness against whatever the future may bring.

'And so I spend my time in working, except for interruptions caused by the time which I have to give just now to festivities in progress, or to those about to take place. But even these disturbances do not bother me much. They rest my mind and although tiring in other ways it is a different kind of fatigue from painting. I wear my full dress for the *Te Deum* services, I attend banquets and enjoy myself as much with fools as with intelligent

10 on 12 pt. Baskerville

Fig. 10. Baskerville set solid and leaded

Historically, Ferdinando Ruano stands at a crucial point of transition between the old writing and the new. Spiritually he belongs to the age of Arrighi and Palatino; but his work represents a break with the rigid, and to some extent arbitrary, punctilios which rendered their styles unpractical and impermanent.

Essentially, that which differentiates italic writing from roman (more properly *antiqua*) whence it sprang, is its informality; and informal it remained from the time of Nicolò Niccoli until the first decade of the

8 pt. Ehrhardt solid

sixteenth century. Then it was that the decorative possibilities of the script were recognized and exploited by trained professional calligraphers who published engraved models, ostensibly for the instruction of the public, but more, in fact, for the display of their own skill and the discomfiture of rivals. The engrafting of formal elements on an informal stock was an inevitable consequence; and from Arrighi's time onwards the *cancellaresca corsiva* (as it was commonly called) became increasingly pointed, narrow, and angular, until in the hands of Palatino it was every whit as

8 on 9 pt. Ehrhardt

spitz-zulaufend and *gitterförmig* as any Gothic text, and scarcely more cursive, in the literal sense of the term. A true cursive implies, as to its parts, the involution in more or less degree of one letter with another; and in the complex the presence of what Mr. Graily Hewitt calls 'a systematic running line'. Systematic Palatino's script certainly is—even to a fault; but of a running line there is little or no trace. The very method of construction is against it. For practical purposes Palatino reduces the chancery alphabet to three basic strokes: horizontal, vertical

8 on 10 pt. Ehrhardt

(or nearly so), and diagonal. Letters and words are formed by the close and careful articulation of these strokes, with an edged pen, rather broad than narrow, cut at a slight angle (*alquanto zoppa*). Ligatures (where permitted) are diagonal hair lines of such a fineness that they could be severed at the point of contact without seriously impairing the integrity of the script. The effect of absolute coherency and discipline is not unpleasing; but the discipline was alien, imposed from without; and it is not easy to see how a script so conceived and expressed could have been made the

8 on 11 pt. Ehrhardt

Fig. 11. Ehrhardt set solid and leaded

Iᴛ is an exhilarating task to evoke the life and personality of
Rubens; good fortune and kindliness abound in him as in hardly
any other great master, and he is well enough known for us to
feel sure of our judgement of him. In the consciousness of his
own noble nature and great powers he must have been one
of the most privileged of mortals. No life is perfect, and
trials came to him too, but the sum of his life so illuminates
all its details that, looked at as a whole, it seems exemplary.
It did not come to a premature end, like that of Masaccio,
Giorgione, or Raphael, while on the other hand he was spared
the weakness of age, and it was in his last years that he created
some of his grandest work. True, from a very early age he met
with advancement on all hands, but not every one could have
taken advantage of it and made men and circumstances serve
him as Rubens did, probably with the greatest composure.

(*a*) Spacing too wide after a full point, resulting in rivers of ob-
    trusive white. There is also a distressing amount of space
    between words compared with space between lines.

Iᴛ is an exhilarating task to evoke the life and personality of
Rubens; good fortune and kindliness abound in him as in hardly
any other great master, and he is well enough known for us to
feel sure of our judgement of him. In the consciousness of his own
noble nature and great powers he must have been one of the most
privileged of mortals. No life is perfect, and trials came to him
too, but the sum of his life so illuminates all its details that, looked
at as a whole, it seems exemplary. It did not come to a premature
end, like that of Masaccio, Giorgione, or Raphael, while on the
other hand he was spared the weakness of age, and it was in his
last years that he created some of his grandest work. True, from
a very early age he met with advancement on all hands, but not
everyone could have taken advantage of it and made men and
circumstances serve him as Rubens did, probably with the greatest
composure.

(*b*) The same as above set more closely with spacing as even as
    possible.

Fig. 12. Example of wide and close setting

Spacing between words should be as even as possible (Fig. 12*b*) if it is desired to avoid rivers of white straggling down the page; and, indeed, even spacing makes an important contribution towards an harmonious-looking page.

Both well-rounded (Baskerville) and heavy (Scotch) type faces permit a little more spacing between the words than do the lighter and more condensed type faces.

Colons, semicolons, quotation, exclamation, and interrogation marks should be separated by an extra hair space from the words they adjoin; this also applies to the spacing between parentheses and the first and terminal letters enclosed when these letters are lower-case ascenders or descenders or capitals with upright stems, e.g. (liberated) not (liberated). Whether in text or display, spacing following a full point needs careful adjustment when the full point follows an abbreviated word or a sloping initial within a sentence, e.g.:

Charles A. Anderson

not   Charles A. Anderson

$2\frac{1}{4}$ in. $\times 5\frac{3}{8}$ in.

not $2\frac{1}{4}$ in. $\times$ $5\frac{3}{8}$ in.

Indention of paragraphs should be one em, but the first paragraph following a heading or subheading should be set full out. Copious extracts should be either indented or set a size or two smaller than the main type of the text (Fig. 13).

There are often special reasons for supporting those who prefer to set copious quotations in smaller type. Poetry that is quoted might conceivably have many overrun lines if set in the same size type as the text; this would be easily avoided if set smaller. Again, many letters quoted in full to give the necessary background to some specific section would result in a book of unnecessary bulk if the letters were printed in the same type size as the text. On the other hand, in a case where the book consists of a collection of letters we might perhaps reverse the procedure and print the letters in the type size chosen for the main text with the editor's commentary set smaller.

Footnotes should be set in type two sizes smaller than the text. The exception to this is found when the printer is limited in his stock to so few sizes of any one type face as to make it impossible. In such cases the text and footnote, being of the same size or nearly so, might advantageously be separated by a thin short metal rule (about two ems long at most) placed to range at the left-hand edge of the type area.

In addition to footnotes, there will be some books with annotations which can only be printed through the use of 'cut-in' or 'hanging shoulder' notes. The former, as their name suggests, are notes printed in a small space cut into the text. The type in which these notes are set must necessarily be very small in size.

The space for hanging shoulder notes is strictly limited, for obvious reasons. The width of the type area available will inevitably be very narrow and lines will tend to be uneven in length. Uneven lines should range on the left for a right-hand page and on the right for a left-hand page on that side of the marginal note which adjoins the text. The first line of a marginal note should be aligned with the relevant lines of text whether the marginal note is set in the same size as the text type or smaller (Fig. 14). When the note is unduly long, it might be necessary to run on part of it at the bottom of the text.

Pagination of the body of the book (exclusive of preliminaries) begins in arabic numerals on the first page of the main text or on the half-title to the text. It is customary for the pagination to be printed centred at the bottom of the text or set on the left and right extremes of the type area either at the bottom of the page or at the top ranged with the head-line. When the pagination is at the top, the numerals are allowed for but not actually printed on the pages of the chapter openings. Similarly, page numbers are not necessarily printed on any full pages of illustrations in the text, particularly when the size of the blocks exceeds the size of the type area.

He never lived in Suffolk again. In 1813 his wife died; for seventeen years she had been ailing and almost out of her mind, yet Crabbe had never ceased to love and cherish her. Before he crossed England to take over a living in Wiltshire, he came back to Aldeburgh for a last visit to one of his sisters. On a lovely day in May he rode over to Parham and Glemham to wander among the fields and woods he loved so well, and to see once more the houses where he and Sarah had spent such happy years. He did not return till late at night, and in his pocket-book were found these lines:

> Yes, I behold again the place,
>   The seat of joy, the source of pain;
> It brings in view the form and face
>   That I must never see again.
>
> The night-bird's song that sweetly floats
>   On this soft gloom—this balmy air,
> Brings to the mind her sweeter notes
>   That I again must never hear.
>
> Lo! yonder shines that window's light,
>   My guide, my token, heretofore;
> And now again it shines as bright,
>   When those dear eyes can shine no more.
>
> Then hurry from this place away!
>   It gives not now the bliss it gave;
> For death has made its charm his prey,
>   And joy is buried in her grave.

With this, one of the best lyrics he ever wrote, I will leave the story of Crabbe, for it concerns Suffolk no more, although, no matter

Fig. 13. Quoted poem set a size smaller than author's prose. In this case it is not done to avoid broken lines but to give clearly to the reader, through surrounding white space, the shape of the poem and its difference in temper from the matter surrounding it.

CHRISTIAN MORALS

that notable King of France* would have his Son to
know but one sentence in Latin, had it been a good one,
perhaps it had been enough. Natural parts and good
Judgments rule the World. States are not governed by
Ergotisms. Many have Ruled well who could not perhaps define a Commonwealth, and they who underſtand
not the Globe of the Earth command a great part of it.
Where natural Logick prevails not, artificial too often
faileth. Where Nature fills the Sails, the Vessel goes
smoothly on, and when Judgment is the Pilot, the
Ensurance need not be high. When Induſtry builds
upon Nature, we may expeĉt Pyramids: where that
foundation is wanting, the ſtruĉture muſt be low. They
do moſt by Books, who could do much without them,
and he that chiefly ows himself unto himself is the
subſtantial Man.

PART II
Lewis the
Eleventh. *Qui
nescit dissimu-
lare nescit
Regnare.*

LET thy Studies be free as thy Thoughts and Contem-
plations, but fly not only upon the wings of Imagination; joyn Sense unto Reason, and Experiment unto
Speculation, and so give life unto Embryon Truths,
and Verities yet in their Chaos. There is nothing more
acceptable unto the Ingenious World, than this noble
Eluĉtation of Truth; wherein, againſt the tenacity of
Prejudice and Prescription, this Century now prevaileth.
What Libraries of new Volumes aftertimes will behold,
and in what a new World of Knowledge the eyes of
our Posterity may be happy, a few Ages may joyfully
declare; and is but a cold thought unto those who
cannot hope to behold this Exantlation of Truth, or
that obscured Virgin half out of the Pit. Which might
make some content with a commutation of the time of
their lives, and to commend the Fancy of the Pytha-
gorean metempsychosis; whereby they might hope to
enjoy this happiness in their third or fourth selves, and
behold that in Pythagoras, which they now but foresee
in Euphorbus*. The World, which took but six days
to make, is like to take six thousand to make out: mean

Section 5

*Ipse ego,
nam memini,
Trojani in tem-
pore belli
Panthoides Eu-
phorbus eram.*
[Ovid, *Metam.*
xv. 160.]

[123]

Fig. 14. Page showing hanging shoulder notes with the uneven
lines ranged inwards.

HEAD-LINES

As already mentioned, the head-lines ('running heads') of a
book are most generally in two parts, the title of the book on
the left-hand page and the chapter title (often of necessity
abbreviated) on the right. The right-hand head-line is, on
occasion, a heading, epitomizing the main subject-matter
of each page, and would consequently be supplied by the
author. The head-line serves several purposes, the most
important being that it enables the reader to pick up a
chapter or section of the book and speedily find a rough
indication of what is in the page. The head-line in the less
ephemeral kind of book is often invaluable when a book
is physically disintegrating, for it then becomes a guide to
future librarians and restorative bookbinders, particularly
if the title or other vital pages of the book are missing.
The head-line imparts typographical character to the page
through the manner and choice of type employed.

Fiction presents a peculiar problem of its own with
regard to head-lines; where they are repeated on both sides
of the page, the effect is tedious. It will be understood,
therefore, why fiction is often printed without head-lines.
In certain books, when there are titles to chapters, it is not
infrequent to have the title of the chapter as the left-hand
head-line, and on the right-hand page a head-line sum-
marizing the main subject-matter on that particular page.

The head-line is most conveniently set in the capitals,
small capitals, or italic of the type face and type size of the
text page. Small capitals are preferable for most books, as
not only do they strike the right degree of emphasis but
they are space-saving in width compared with capitals.
Capitals tend to produce over-emphasis and monotony,
but are nevertheless useful on a large page and when the
words of the head-line are short. Capitals and small capitals
should be letter-spaced to attain full legibility. Head-lines
should be separated from the text by a nonpareil (two
thick leads) white space or the equivalent depth of a line of
the type in which the book is set.

The use of italic capitals for short head-lines presents many subtleties and difficulties, and we take this opportunity of examining italic capitals in general. In Fig. 15 on the following page, we have the words *TRANSVAAL LAWYER REPRIEVED* set in 12 pt. italic capitals in seven of the type faces shown on pages 14 and 15. These italic capitals are set both close and letter-spaced. It is obvious immediately that the slope of the italic capitals is more even throughout in some type faces and irregular in others. If a book is set in Baskerville, Times, Imprint or other types with a fairly even slope to all the letters, it would be reasonable to set headlines in italic capitals if desired, but it would be inadvisable in Bell, Caslon, Garamond, or Walbaum, and types with similar very irregular slope to the italic capitals, even when the capitals are letter-spaced; the sharp fall-away of the *A* and *W* presents an inharmonious effect disturbing to the eye of the most unsophisticated reader. These types, in fact, were never designed with the purpose in view of setting whole words in italic capitals.[1]

The Perpetua and Times italics are more closely related to their roman than any other types; their italics might be called a sloping roman. The Baskerville italic is mildly decorative by the nature of its seven dandified capital letters, the *J K N Q T Y* and *Z* which border on being swash letters, and it is curious that no alternative letters were designed by Baskerville.

Head-lines set in capitals and lower-case italic can look agreeable, while plain rules supporting the head-lines can, on occasion, add variety and richness to a page (Fig. 16).

[1] See 'Towards an Ideal Italic', by Stanley Morison. *The Fleuron*, No. v. 1926.

BASKERVILLE

TRANSVAAL LAWYER REPRIEVED

TRANSVAAL LAWYER REPRIEVED

BELL

TRANSVAAL LAWYER REPRIEVED

TRANSVAAL LAWYER REPRIEVED

BEMBO

TRANSVAAL LAWYER REPRIEVED

TRANSVAAL LAWYER REPRIEVED

CASLON

TRANSVAAL LAWYER REPRIEVED

TRANSVAAL LAWYER REPRIEVED

EHRHARDT

TRANSVAAL LAWYER REPRIEVED

TRANSVAAL LAWYER REPRIEVED

PERPETUA

TRANSVAAL LAWYER REPRIEVED

TRANSVAAL LAWYER REPRIEVED

TIMES

TRANSVAAL LAWYER REPRIEVED

TRANSVAAL LAWYER REPRIEVED

Fig. 15. Italic capitals closely set and letter-spaced

How things bind and blend themselves together! The last time I saw the Fountain of Trevi, it was from Arthur's father's room—Joseph Severn's, where we both took Joanie to see him in 1872, and the old man made a sweet drawing of his pretty daughter-in-law, now in her schoolroom; he himself then eager in finishing his last picture of the Marriage in Cana, which he had caused to take place under a vine trellis, and delighted himself by painting the crystal and ruby glittering of the changing rivulet of water out of the Greek vase, glowing into wine. Fonte Branda I last saw with Charles Norton, under the same arches where Dante saw it. We drank of it together, and walked together that evening on the hills above, where the fireflies among the scented thickets shone fitfully in the still undarkened air. *How* they shone! moving like fine-broken starlight through the purple leaves. How they shone! through the sunset that faded into thunderous night as I entered Siena three days before, the white edges of the mountainous clouds still lighted from the west, and the openly golden sky calm behind the Gate of Siena's heart, with its still golden words, "Cor magis tibi Sena pandit," and the fireflies everywhere in the sky and cloud rising and falling, mixed with the lightning, and more intense than the stars.

BRANTWOOD
    June 19th, 1889.

Fig. 16. Page showing head-line
enlivened by a rule.

THE CHAPTER OPENING

The chapter heading most commonly consists of the number of the chapter followed by the title. The chapter
number may either consist of a plain (II, 2, 2) numeral or
it may be preceded by the word CHAPTER. When there is
a chapter title as well, this title takes first place in the
reader's interest and should be set more prominently than
the chapter number (or the head-line), e.g.:

CHAPTER I

THE VOLUNTARY EXILE

Both the chapter number and title are displayed lines
and do not, therefore, require punctuation.

If the word CHAPTER is set in capitals, roman
numerals should be used, unless the fount possesses
modern numerals which range with the capitals, e.g.:

CHAPTER II (Walbaum with roman numeral)

CHAPTER 2 (Times with modern numeral)

not CHAPTER 2 (Walbaum with old style numeral)

It will readily be seen that an old style numeral in juxtaposition with capitals presents an awkward appearance.

A book is divided into chapters partly to provide a series
of breaks which assist the reader by giving him a convenient amount of reading at a stretch, which he can adapt
to his powers of concentration and the amount of time at
his disposal. Each chapter should, therefore, begin on a
fresh page (left or right) and, to make this beginning
doubly clear, it is a useful convention which causes a new
chapter opening to be dropped a few lines down the page.
An exception may be made in pocket editions and when
condensation is imperative, in which case the chapter
heading can run on without starting a new page (Fig. 18).
The first word of the text of a new chapter requires special

typographical treatment. The first word, which should not be indented, can most commonly be set either in:

(*a*) Capitals
(*b*) Small Capitals
(*c*) Capitals and Small Capitals.

(*a*) Capitals are satisfactory in a type where the capitals range lower than the ascenders, as in Bembo and Perpetua, but, in most other types, the use of capitals for the opening word of a chapter tends to over-emphasis.

(*b*) Conversely, small capitals tend towards understatement unless used in conjunction with an initial letter.

(*c*) Capitals and small capitals strike a good medium and are, perhaps, the most convenient for the the first word of the chapter opening in the average book. Whichever of the above alternatives is adopted, the capitals and small capitals should be letter-spaced.

SOME people have a foolish way of not minding, or pretending not to mind, what they eat. For my part, I mind my belly very studiously, and very carefully; for I look upon it, that he who does not mind his belly will hardly mind anything else.

(a) 10 on 11 pt. Bembo, opening in capitals

DEPEND upon it that if a man talks of his misfortunes there is something in them that is not disagreeable to him, for where there is nothing but pure misery, there is never any recourse to the mention of it.

(b) 10 on 11 pt. Plantin, opening in small capitals

EVERY man who comes into the world has need of friends. If he has to get them for himself, half his life is spent before his merit is known. Relations are a man's ready friends who support him. When a man is in real distress, he flies into the arms of his relations.

(c) 10 on 11 pt. Ehrhardt, opening in capitals and small capitals

Fig. 17

Where the first word of a chapter is a single letter, i.e.
A or I, it is desirable to include in the display the word
following in order to balance the initial.

Initial letters emphasize a chapter opening to a marked
degree. They can be either raised or dropped. The most
simple raised initial is a capital letter of the text type set
two sizes larger, but some printers have types that impart
a more decorative effect. All dropped initial letters must
appear to range with the lines of the matter which adjoins,
and spacing to the right must be regulated according to
the shape of the letter. The remaining letters of the word
will generally be set in capitals or small capitals to support
the initial whether it is raised or dropped. In all cases
initials must fit snugly (Fig. 20 (*a*) and (*b*)). Dropped
initials need to be of a certain size to achieve an agreeable
effect, therefore when they are used with 11 pt. type or
under, it would be unwise to use them smaller than three-
line. The capitals of a good type with the beard filed off
make adequate initial letters if the printer has no initial
letters in his stock (Fig. 21).

An initial letter is, on occasion, used for the opening
chapter of the book only. Certainly the opening of the
main text of a book is made unmistakably clear by such
emphasis. But this emphasis can also be achieved either by
printing the title or an abbreviated title of the book at the
top of the opening page, above the chapter number, or by
introducing a second half-title page on the last right-hand
page preceding the opening of the main text.

In any case care must be exercised to ensure that an
initial letter does not strike a discordant note on the opening page of the text when the title of the book is also
displayed in the upper portion of the page. If the display is
simply set in the text type, an initial, even a highly decorative initial, can generally be safely used. On the other
hand if the title is set in a decorative or semi-decorative
type, or in some special manner, it would be well not to
use a dropped initial letter at all.

She instantly let go his hand and changed colour. Their eyes met: his almost frenzied gaze was fixed upon her; it was not Oblomov but passion itself looked at her. Olga understood that his words had escaped him involuntarily and that they were true.

He came to himself, picked up his hat, and ran out of the room without turning round. She did not follow him with questioning eyes; she stood for several minutes by the piano, motionless as a statue, her eyes fixed on the ground, her bosom heaving.

VI

WHENEVER Oblomov lay idly absorbed in drowsy stupor or in flights of fancy, in the foreground of his dreams always stood a woman—his wife, never his mistress. In his dreams he saw the image of a tall, graceful woman, with gentle yet proud eyes and a dreamy expression, her head gracefully poised on her shoulders, her arms serenely folded on her breast as she sat in an easy attitude among the creepers on the balcony or stepped lightly on the carpets or on the sandy avenues, her waist swaying as she walked; she was his ideal, the embodiment of a whole life filled with ease and serene repose, she was peace itself. He dreamed of her first at the altar wearing a long veil and wreathed in flowers, at the head of the marriage-bed with her eyes shyly cast down, then as a mother among a group of children. He dreamed of her smile, not a smile of passion, but of sympathetic understanding for him, her husband, and of indulgence for others; he dreamed of her eyes, not moist with passion, but kind only to him

251

Fig. 18. An occasion when a chapter opening
is not given a new page.

CHAPTER VII

Ecclesiastical architecture in the Netherlands—The image-breaking—Description of Antwerp Cathedral—Ceremony of the Ommegang—Precursory disturbances—Iconoclasts at Antwerp—Incidents of the image-breaking in various cities—Events at Tournay—Preaching of Wille—Disturbance by a little boy—Churches sacked at Tournay—Disinterment of Duke Adolphus of Gueldres—Iconoclasts defeated and massacred at Anchin—Bartholomew's day at Valenciennes—General characteristics of the image-breaking—Testimony of contemporaries as to the honesty of the rioters—Consternation of the Duchess—Projected flight to Mons—Advice of Horn and other seigniors—Accord of 25th August.

THE Netherlands possessed an extraordinary number of churches and monasteries. Their exquisite architecture and elaborate decoration had been the earliest indication of intellectual culture displayed in the country. In the vast number of cities, towns, and villages which were crowded upon that narrow territory, there had been, from circumstances operating throughout Christendom, a great accumulation of ecclesiastical wealth. The same causes can never exist again which at an early day covered the soil of Europe with those magnificent creations of Christian art. It was in these anonymous but entirely original achievements that Gothic genius, awaking from its long sleep of the dark ages, first expressed itself. The early poetry of the German races was hewn and chiselled in stone. Around the steadfast principle of devotion then so firmly rooted in the soil, clustered the graceful and vigorous emanations of the newly-awakened mind. All that science could invent, all that art could embody, all that mechanical ingenuity could dare, all that wealth could lavish,—whatever there was of human energy which was panting for pacific utterance, wherever there stirred the vital principle which instinctively strove to create and to adorn at an epoch when vulgar violence and destructiveness were the general tendencies of humanity, all gathered around these magnificent temples, as their aspiring pinnacles at last pierced the mist which had so long brooded over the world.

Fig. 19. Chapter opening from Motley's *The Rise of the Dutch Republic* with synopsis of chapter contents.

THE Revelation of Jesus Christ, which God gave unto him, to shew unto his servants things which must shortly come to pass; and he sent and signified it by his angel unto his servant John: ¶ 2 Who bare record of the word of God, and of the testimony of Jesus Christ, and of all

(*a*) Five-line initial. The serif of the left arm of the T overlaps the type measure, resulting in the initial being placed correctly *optically*.

ALMIGHTY God, our heavenly Father, who of his great mercy hath promised forgiveness of sins to all them that with hearty repentance and true faith turn unto him;

(*b*) Three-line initial with the serif of the left tail of the A overlapping the type measure, resulting in the initial being placed correctly *optically*. The remainder of the word in capitals is drawn in towards the initial, as always in the case of a dropped initial A.

WE do not presume to come to this thy Table, O merciful Lord, trusting in our own righteousness, but in thy manifold and great mercies. We are not worthy so much as to gather up the crumbs under thy

(*c*) Ill-fitting initial. The initial falls below the third line and is consequently neither a three- nor a four-line initial. The left-hand serif does not overlap the type measure.

Fig. 20

A B C D E F

Caslon Titling

H I J K L M

Lyons Titling

N O P Q R

Bembo Titling

H I J L M N

Old Face Open Titling

A B C D E

Perpetua Titling

Fig. 21. Examples of types suitable for initials: titling, which has
no beard at the foot, or capitals with the beard removed.

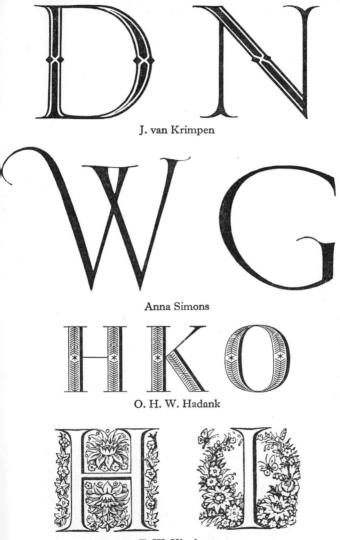

J. van Krimpen

Anna Simons

O. H. W. Hadank

F. W. Kleukens

Fig. 22. A selection of decorative initial letters

THE PRINTING OF PLAYS

The setting of a play has its own typographical necessities. Whilst the choice of type and the margins of the page are subject to the same principles as the printing of prose, it is of primary importance to be able to pick out the part of each character with speed, and the stage directions should be clearly differentiated from the rest of the text. The names of the different characters can be set either in capitals and lower-case italic, capitals and small capitals, or in even small capitals at the beginning of the line, but in each case the text following should be indented. This indention of the part throws the player's name into strong relief. The stage directions should be in italic. Square brackets are used to enclose stage directions when these appear within the dialogue (Fig. 24). The head-line should include the number of the act and the scene number, when there is more than one scene in the act. When a play is printed for reading rather than for use by actors, the names of the characters may be centred above the part to be spoken (Fig. 25). This method will undoubtedly result in a handsome page for leisurely reading, but it results, too, in a longer book. In this case the names of characters should be set in capitals or small capitals to ensure that there will be no possibility of confusion with any stage directions set in italic.

It is rarely necessary for a play to be printed with a table of contents. Instead it is usual to print a *Dramatis Personae* which consists of a list of the characters with the addition, when relevant, of their ranks, professions, etc., and their relation to each other, viz:

> BASILIO, *King of Poland*
> SEGISMUNDO, *Basilio's son*
> ASTOLFO, *Duke of Muscovy*
> CLOTALDO, *Segismundo's keeper*
> CLARIN, *Servant to Rosaura*
> ESTRELLA, *Basilio's niece*
> ROSAURA, *A lady of Muscovy*

That yet you do not know. Fie on this storm,
I will go seek the King.

GENTLEMAN: Give me your hand, have you no more to
say?

KENT: Few words, but to effect more than all yet;
That when we have found the King, in which your pain
That way, I'll this: he that first lights on him,
Holla the other.

Exeunt.

III. 2

Storm still.
Enter Lear, and Fool.

LEAR: Blow winds, and crack your cheeks; rage, blow
You cataracts, and hurricanoes spout,
Till you have drench'd our steeples, drown'd the cocks.
You sulphurous and thought-executing fires,
Vaunt-couriers of oak-cleaving thunderbolts,
Singe my white head. And thou all-shaking thunder,
Strike flat the thick rotundity o' th' world,
Crack Nature's moulds, all germens spill at once
That makes ingrateful man.

FOOL: O nuncle, Court holy-water in a dry house, is better
than this rain-water out o' door. Good nuncle, in, ask thy
daughter's blessing; here's a night pities neither wise
men, nor fools.

LEAR: Rumble thy bellyful: spit fire, spout rain:
Nor rain, wind, thunder, fire are my daughters;
I tax not you, you elements with unkindness.
I never gave you Kingdom, call'd you children;
You owe me no subscription. Then let fall
Your horrible pleasure. Here I stand your slave,

Fig. 23. Page from play in prose and verse. Head-line displays both
act and scene number. Large type is used for commencement of
new scene (arabic numeral), with the number of the act repeated
(roman numeral).

ACT TWO

NINA. For the bliss of being a writer or an actress I could endure want, and disillusionment, and the hatred of my friends, and the pangs of my own dissatisfaction with myself; but I should demand in return fame, real, resounding fame! [*She covers her face with her hands*] Whew! My head reels!

THE VOICE OF ARKADINA. [*From inside the house*] Boris! Boris!

TRIGORIN. She is calling me, probably to come and pack, but I don't want to leave this place. [*His eyes rest on the lake*] What a blessing such beauty is!

NINA. Do you see that house there, on the far shore?

TRIGORIN. Yes.

NINA. That was my dead mother's home. I was born there, and have lived all my life beside this lake. I know every little island in it.

TRIGORIN. This is a beautiful place to live. [*He catches sight of the dead seagull*] What is that?

NINA. A gull. Constantine shot it.

TRIGORIN. What a lovely bird! Really, I can't bear to go away. Can't you persuade Irina to stay? [*He writes something in his note-book.*]

NINA. What are you writing?

TRIGORIN. Nothing much, only an idea that occurred to me. [*He puts the book back in his pocket*] An idea for a short story. A young girl grows up on the shores of a lake, as you have. She loves the lake as the gulls do, and is as happy and free as they. But a man sees her who chances to come that way, and he destroys her out of idleness, as this gull here has been destroyed.
A pause. ARKADINA *appears at one of the windows.*

Fig. 24. Setting of play in prose. Square brackets used only when directions appear within the dialogue. Text indented so that each character speaking can be quickly picked out.

BOSOLA

In a mist: I know not how,
Such a mistake, as I have often seene
In a play: Oh, I am gone—
We are onely like dead wals, or vaulted graves,
That ruin'd, yeildes no eccho: Fare you well—
It may be paine: but no harme to me to die,
In so good a quarrell: Oh this gloomy world,
In what a shadow, or deepe pit of darknesse,
Doth (womanish, and fearefull) mankind live!
Let worthy mindes nere stagger in distrust
To suffer death, or shame, for what is just—
Mine is another voyage.

PESCARA

The noble *Delio*, as I came to th' Pallace,
Told me of *Antonio's* being here, and shew'd me
A pritty gentleman his sonne and heire.
                              [*Enter Delio with Antonio's Son*

MALLATESTE

Oh Sir, you come to[o] late.

DELIO

I heard so, and
Was arm'd for 't ere I came: Let us make noble use
Of this great ruine; and joyne all our force
To establish this yong hopefull Gentleman
In 's mothers right. These wretched eminent things
Leave no more fame behind 'em, then should one
Fall in a frost, and leave his print in snow—
As soone as the sun shines, it ever melts,
Both forme, and matter: I have ever thought
Nature doth nothing so great, for great men,
As when she's pleas'd to make them Lords of truth:
    '*Integrity of life, is fames best friend,*
Which noblely (beyond Death) shall crowne the end.'

Fig. 25. Page from a play, with characters centred

THE PRINTING OF POETRY

The printing of poetry is more complex than the printing of prose, and any rules must allow for many exceptions. Poetry is more slowly and deliberately read than prose, which means that the reader is more than usually aware of typographical qualities. The choice of a good type face and its point size is governed by the importance of avoiding broken lines, therefore the types with a narrow set, and in relatively small sizes, are the most suitable, such as Bembo, Caslon, Ehrhardt, Fournier, Times, and Walbaum. Type that is too large is a disadvantage because it means that the shape of the poem may be lost, and the shape of a poem is not only pleasing to the eye, but is a help to the mind in grasping the rhythmic character of the poem. This is important in much contemporary poetry when no traditional metrical scheme is followed. Even when using types small in point size and narrow in set, it is sometimes necessary to exceed the type measure for an occasional line to avoid a break. In the setting of poetry all types should be leaded

(*a*) WHAT dire Offence from am'rous Causes springs,
     What mighty contests rise from trivial Things,
     I sing—This verse to CARYL, Muse! is due;
     This, ev'n *Belinda* may vouchsafe to view;
     Slight is the Subject, but not so the Praise,
     If She inspire, and He approve, my Lays.

(*b*) WHAT dire Offence from am'rous Causes springs,
     What mighty contests rise from trivial Things,
     I sing—This verse to CARYL, Muse! is due;
     This, ev'n *Belinda* may vouchsafe to view;
     Slight is the Subject, but not so the Praise,
     If She inspire, and He approve, my Lays.

(*a*) Set in 10 on 11 pt. Bembo close set, middle space between the words.

(*b*) Set in 10 on 11 pt. Baskerville, wide set, thick space between the words.

Fig. 26

and spacing between the words should be even; a middle
space between each word. If the setting is amply leaded
the space between the words may be increased (Fig. 26),
particularly when the type is wide on the body. Short-line
poems should be indented to balance the margins, and the
title of each poem should be centred on the *optical* centre
of the poem, not on the first line, two very important
points and a test of skill to the compositor. The shape of
stanza forms should always be apparent on the page;
where possible, in case of lyric poetry, the whole poem
should be on a single page, but if this is impossible the
break must be made between stanzas and not in the middle
of a stanza. The space between stanzas depends, to a certain
extent, on the amount of room to spare when the page is
made up.

It is generally impracticable to incorporate running
head-lines except where the book consists of one or two
long poems. Where the book is an anthology, the reader
likes to be able to pick out easily the contribution of each
poet. Each author's name can be set as a shoulder note in
the outer margins which would fulfil, in effect, a similar
purpose to a head-line. The disadvantages are that shoulder
notes take more time to compose and arrange and the
margins must be on the generous side.

Folios are best at the bottom, either to the left or right of
the page or centred. In cases where the poems themselves
are numbered and where the folios are centred, the folios
might well be enclosed in brackets.

The beginning of each poem is the equivalent of a new
chapter opening in prose, and may have similar ceremonial
treatment, such as raised or dropped initial letters or the
first word of each poem set in capitals and small capitals.
A dropped initial letter is most conveniently used when
poems are set full out, as in the case of blank verse, heroic
couplets, and the Shakespearian sonnet: on the other hand
a dropped initial letter tends to be disturbing if used with
poems which include indented lines at their beginnings,
or if the verse is short.

The printer should follow the poet's MS. for capitalization. If capitals are not used to begin every fresh line
then they should only be used where indicated by the poet,
either for emphasis or for punctuation (i.e. sense). When
no punctuation is used and capitals are only used to
indicate the beginning of a new sentence, it would avoid
possible confusion if initial capitals were *not* used invariably
at the beginning of each line.

Each line is set full out in heroic couplets, half-rhymes,
the Shakespearian sonnet (Fig. 27), and blank verse.
Quatrains of alternately four and three stress lines should
not be set full out, nor should short lines in other stanza
forms be set full out *where the shape of the stanza is
important.*[1] Indention does not depend so much on rhyme
but on length of line and consequent appearance of the
poem. Short lines appearing in poems that are in the main
decasyllabic are consequently indented.

LIKE as the waves make towards the pebbled shore,
    So do our minutes hasten to their end;
Each changing place with that which goes before,
.In secret toil all forwards do contend.
Nativity, once in the main of light,
Crawls to maturity, wherewith being crown'd,
Crooked eclipses 'gainst his glory fight,
And Time that gave doth now his gift confound.
Time doth transfix the flourish set on youth
And delves the parallels in beauty's brow,
Feeds on the rarities of nature's truth,
And nothing stands but for his scythe to mow:
    And yet to times in hope my verse shall stand,
    Praising thy worth, despite his cruel hand.

Fig. 27. Shakespearian sonnet with a dropped initial
and last two rhymed lines indented.

[1] 'For the very look of verse on the printed page excites definite
expectations in the mind of the reader, just as a glimpse at a bill of
fare excites certain digestive juices in one's body.' From *The
Printing of Poetry*, by Walter de la Mare. 1931.

TO LEIGH HUNT

A DEDICATION

GLORY and loveliness have pass'd away;
  For if we wander out in early morn,
  No wreathed incense do we see upborne
Into the east, to meet the smiling day:
No crowd of nymphs soft voic'd and young, and gay,
  In woven baskets bringing ears of corn,
  Roses, and pinks, and violets, to adorn
The shrine of Flora in her early May.
But there are left delights as high as these,
  And I shall ever bless my destiny,
That in a time, when under pleasant trees
  Pan is no longer sought, I feel a free,
A leafy luxury, seeing I could please
  With these poor offerings, a man like thee.

Fig. 28. Sonnet by Keats with variation of sequence of rhymes on the same sound. Lines 1, 4, 5 and 8 rhyme on the same sound, lines 2, 3, 6 and 7 on another and are set indented. There is no rhymed couplet at the end.

THOU hast made me, and shall Thy work decay?
Repair me now, for now mine end doth haste;
I run to death, and death meets me as fast,
And all my pleasures are like yesterday.
I dare not move my dim eyes any way;
Despair behind, and death before doth cast
Such terror, and my feeble flesh doth waste
By sin in it, which it t'wards hell doth weigh.
Only Thou art above, and when towards Thee
By Thy leave I can look, I rise again;
But our old subtle foe so tempteth me,
That not one hour myself I can sustain;
Thy Grace may wing me to prevent his art,
And Thou like adamant draw mine iron heart.

Fig. 29. Sonnet by John Donne, set in the same manner as the Shakespearian sonnet, but without indented couplet at the end.

FROM 'TO HIS COY MISTRESS'

HAD we but world enough, and time,
This coyness, lady, were no crime.
We would sit down, and think which way
To walk, and pass our long love's day.
Thou by the Indian Ganges' side
Should'st rubies find: I by the tide
Of Humber would complain. I would
Love you ten years before the Flood:
And you should if you please refuse
Till the conversion of the Jews.
My vegetable love should grow
Vaster than empires, and more slow.
An hundred years should go to praise
Thine eyes, and on thy forehead gaze.
Two hundred to adore each breast:
But thirty thousand to the rest.

Fig. 30. Lyrical verse by Andrew Marvell in a simple metrical scheme with lines rhyming in couples, all set full out.

FROM 'LOVE LIVES BEYOND THE TOMB'

Love lives beyond
The tomb, the earth, which fades like dew!
I love the fond,
The faithful, and the true.

Love lives in sleep,
The happiness of healthy dreams:
Eve's dews may weep,
But love delightful seems.

Tis seen in flowers,
And in the morning's pearly dew;
In earth's green hours,
And in the heaven's eternal blue.

Fig. 31. Lyrical verse by John Clare in a simple metrical scheme with alternate rhymed lines indented.

WE'LL GO NO MORE A-ROVING

So, we'll go no more a-roving
 So late into the night,
Though the heart be still as loving,
 And the moon be still as bright.

For the sword outwears its sheath,
 And the soul wears out the breast,
And the heart must pause to breathe,
 And love itself have rest.

Though the night was made for loving,
 And the day returns too soon,
Yet we'll go no more a-roving
 By the light of the moon.

Fig. 32. Ballad by Byron, alternate rhymed lines indented

FROM 'CHRISTENDOM'

Things native sweetly grew,
 Which there mine eye did view,
Plain, simple, cheap, on either side the street,
 Which was exceeding fair and wide;
 Sweet mansions there mine eyes did meet,
 Green trees the shaded doors did hide:
  My chiefest joys
  Were girls and boys
That in those streets still up and down did play,
Which crown'd the Town with constant holiday.

Fig. 33. Example of an irregularly set verse from a poem by
Thomas Traherne.

5

THE PRELIMINARY PAGES

THE preliminary pages, technically known as 'Prelims', are a very important section of a book and include all the introductory pages preceding the main text. Prelims are sometimes few, consisting of, perhaps, a half-title, title, imprint, and contents pages, or they may comprise considerably more items occupying many pages made up of half-title, title, history of the book and printer's imprint, dedication, acknowledgements, contents, list of illustrations, preface, introduction, and corrigenda or errata. (For order of Prelims see page 8.)

The Prelims are set and made up after the galley proofs of the text have been put into final form in page proof, and it has consequently been ascertained that there are no further corrections or additions to be made nor any alterations in the pagination. Text pages are paginated in ordinary figures (arabic) 1, 2, 3, etc., whilst roman lower-case numerals are used for the pagination of the Prelims, i, ii, iii, iv, etc.

This separation in the manner of the pagination is most useful. The Introduction, for instance, is usually written when the book is in its final page form, so that the page references and quotations taken from the text by the writer of the Introduction to clarify his meaning can be verified. Likewise, the Contents Page and List of Illustrations can only be completed when the pagination of the text is complete. The Corrigenda is the final operation, for it makes its regrettable but sometimes necessary appearance after the body of the book has been printed.

The division of the pagination serves other useful purposes. The body of the book can go to press whilst the Prelims are being compiled, set, and proofed. The Prelims themselves can be subject to alteration or addition until they go to press without risking the expense and entailing the inconvenience of repaginating the whole book.

THE HALF-TITLE

From the point of view of the reader, the title-page is the first page of interest in a book, and, at a first glance, the half-title might appear to be superfluous. But the half-title fulfils useful purposes. It must be printed with the Prelims, and this ensures that the paper of the page facing the title-page is of the same kind as the rest of the book and not a page of the endpapers. The half-title page also protects the title-page from any glue or its chemical constituents which may percolate through from the binding boards, and it helps, in general, to protect the title-page during the various stages of binding. The half-title plays a modest and strictly utilitarian part, and needs very simple typographic display. Usually the title of the book only is set in capitals in the same size of the type used in the text, set centred or to the right, well above the optical centre of the page. If it is desired to print a list of works previously published by an author, this can conveniently be printed on the verso of the half-title, neatly displayed in small type.

THE TITLE-PAGE

The title-page has been a prominent typographic feature of the book ever since printing emerged from the *incunabula* period. It not only lends itself to skill and variety of typographical treatment but reflects the typographic quality of the whole book, and it is no accident that a third of the five hundred or so plates of Mr. Stanley Morison's monumental *Four Centuries of Fine Printing* should display title-pages. Moreover the same author has stated in his *First Principles of Typography* that 'The history of printing is in a large measure the history of the title-page'.

During the present century title-pages have become noticeably simpler both in their display and in the economy of words used. Striking and decorative emphasis appears now to centre on the book-jacket, which has attained a far greater importance than ever before as a means of advertisement and as an immediate attraction to the bookseller and book buyer. But the book-jacket is a transitory thing, liable to become quickly soiled, torn, or removed and, therefore, serves only to give a pleasing first impression. Simple or elaborate, the title-page holds an assured place for the serious buyer, both for the information it gives and for the permanent degree to which it attracts the owner and reader of the book by its typographic style, with or without graphic ornamentation.

The title-page most commonly displays, in the following order, the title of the book, the name of the author, the publisher's imprint with place and date of publication.[1]

This is usually the minimum amount of information that must be given, but often a title-page must show considerably more, including a subtitle, editor, translator, illustrator, number of plates, number of volumes, and a quotation. Where a book extends into separate volumes, the complete number of volumes should be stated if this is known in advance as well as the actual volume number of each book (Fig. 34).

THE DISPLAY

The title and subtitle of a book are the most emphasized feature of a title-page display, followed by the name of the author and gradually diminishing in emphasis down to the address of the publisher and the place and date of publication, set in graduated sizes of type according to the relative importance of the items to be displayed. There are some exceptions. For instance, in the case of a particular translation from a Latin or Greek classic, as the *Iliad* of Homer, translated by Alexander Pope, the name of the translator should have the typographical prominence usually given to the author.

But in general, the title, subtitle, and name of the author should be set in capitals or small capitals. Small capitals,

[1] Some publishers prefer the date of publication to be on the verso of the title-page. The reason for this appears to be that where a new book has remained in the bookshop unsold for some time, this distressing fact might escape immediate notice.

The Zohar

TRANSLATED BY HARRY SPERLING
MAURICE SIMON
AND DR. PAUL P. LEVERTOFF

FIVE VOLUMES
III

LONDON
THE SONCINO PRESS
5 Gower Street
1933

Fig. 34. Title-page of a publication in five volumes,
clearly stating the fact.

and lower case with roman and italic, are at the printer's disposal for display of subsidiary matter, in addition to capitals in small sizes.

The main word of the title should not be broken, although the article attached to the word chosen for the largest size of display may be set in a separate line in the same sized type or smaller, and there are other occasions when this can be done.

It is on the whole an admirable tradition that the main headings of the title-page are set in sizes larger than the size of the capital of the text; it lends unmistakable clarity to the page, and taken in conjunction with the subsidiary matter (some of which might be smaller in size than the text) it enables the title-page to have an harmonious link with the text pages. Care should be taken not to set the main display in too large a size, and here perhaps there is a partial check owing to the desirability of avoiding broken words. No other word or line in a book should be set larger than the largest size of type on the title-page.

The basic arrangement of a title-page is conditioned by the wording, and by this we mean the number of words and their length, together with the number of items to be displayed. It is as well, therefore, to have no preconceived ideas of a style, and attempts should be resisted to force squared (broad) asymmetrical or tapered (triangular) effects. Where there is very little wording to be set, the title-page (if unornamented and set in reasonable display sizes) will contain a large amount of white space between the upper part—title and author—and the lower part—publisher and place. This is quite natural and within its limits can be treated through the right juxtaposition of type sizes, coupled with meticulous spacing of letters and lines displayed in the right position on the page (Fig. 41).

The graduated sizes of the types used, coupled with the clarity of a title-page setting as a whole, make it unnecessary to have full points at the end of display lines. These would serve no useful purpose, while their inclusion would throw out of harmony the visual balance of the lines.

This is, admittedly, only a rough guide for the setting of the title-page, which, in its details, obviously invites great variation in its treatment.

SPACING AND LEADING

Capitals should be letter-spaced, but without exaggeration, and the spacing between letters should never be as much as the amount of white space (leading) between lines.

Letter-spacing undoubtedly enhances the legibility of lines or words of capitals. I M N H U have upright stems, whilst A B C D E F G J K L O P Q R S T V W X Y Z have curved, angular or broken stems. When letters of these two categories come up against each other, awkward gaps of white space or undue cramping are presented to the eye which can be obviated by letter-spacing, e.g.

IRRAWADDY RIVER

not IRRAWADDY RIVER (without letter-spacing).

A title-page contains relatively few lines, and is composed in any case by hand, so the time factor does not press unduly. Thus the letter-spacing can and should be done by hand. This will enable the compositor to do all that is necessary to letter-space correctly the many combinations of capital letters that might occur. The letter I, for instance, needs still more space to the left of it in the combination N I than it does in the combination R I, and so on *ad infinitum*. The above also applies to small capitals.

The leading between lines plays a big part in title-page display. It aids in the throwing of specific words or lines into relief, and is essential between lines of letter-spaced capitals, to enable the capitals to be displayed with the maximum clarity. There should, as we have already remarked, always be more white space between lines than between letters and words. Furthermore, leading affects the 'colour' and balance of the title-page (Fig. 38). De Vinne has rightly asserted that 'compactness makes

NIMPHIDIA

THE COURT OF
FAYRIE

BY MICHAEL DRAYTON

STRATFORD–UPON–AVON
AT THE SHAKESPEARE HEAD
OXFORD BASIL BLACKWELL
MCMXXI

Fig. 35. Title-page with main display in black
and all subsidiary matter in red.

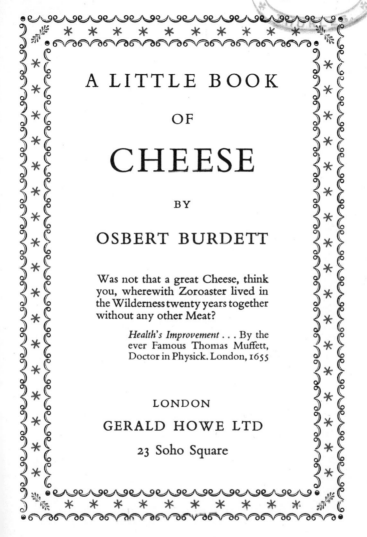

A LITTLE BOOK

OF

CHEESE

BY

OSBERT BURDETT

Was not that a great Cheese, think
you, wherewith Zoroaster lived in
the Wilderness twenty years together
without any other Meat?

Health's Improvement . . . By the
ever Famous Thomas Muffett,
Doctor in Physick. London, 1655

LONDON

GERALD HOWE LTD

23 Soho Square

Fig. 36. Decorative title-page with border that does not
overpower the type displayed.

confusion. The compositor who sets a title-page will soon learn that it is the relief of white space, as much as the largeness of type, that produces the readability.'

IMPOSITION

We have already discussed the imposition of text pages, and in our illustrations on pages 22 and 23 we have shown that a page opening is an entity. The title-page, on the other hand, is a single right-hand page and thus needs a different imposition.

The top and bottom margins will be uniform with the text pages, but the inner and outer margins will differ from the text in that the inner margin will be increased a little and the outer decreased proportionately (Fig. 37).

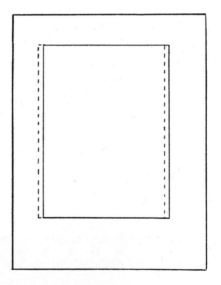

Fig. 37. Imposition for title-page.
Dotted lines represent position of text.

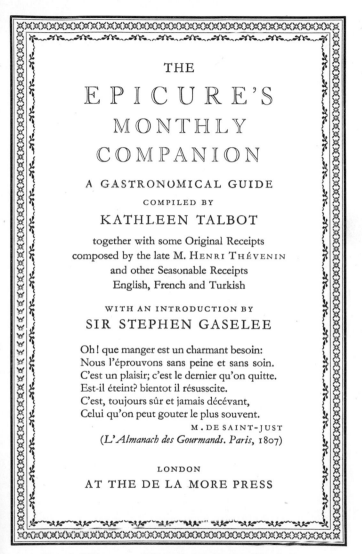

THE
EPICURE'S
MONTHLY
COMPANION

A GASTRONOMICAL GUIDE

COMPILED BY

KATHLEEN TALBOT

together with some Original Receipts
composed by the late M. HENRI THÉVENIN
and other Seasonable Receipts
English, French and Turkish

WITH AN INTRODUCTION BY
SIR STEPHEN GASELEE

Oh! que manger est un charmant besoin:
Nous l'éprouvons sans peine et sans soin.
C'est un plaisir; c'est le dernier qu'on quitte.
Est-il éteint? bientot il résusscite.
C'est, toujours sûr et jamais décévant,
Celui qu'on peut gouter le plus souvent.

M. DE SAINT-JUST
(*L'Almanach des Gourmands. Paris*, 1807)

LONDON
AT THE DE LA MORE PRESS

Fig. 38. Title-page with ample wording, well leaded and
showing subtle contrasts in type sizes.

Nineteenth Century Poetry

AN ANTHOLOGY CHOSEN BY
JOHN HAYWARD

1950

Chatto & Windus

LONDON

Fig. 39. Title-page with well-placed device,
harmonizing with the type.

THE NOVEL LIBRARY

THE HISTORY OF

THE LIFE OF THE LATE MR.

JONATHAN WILD

THE GREAT

BY

HENRY FIELDING

LONDON

HAMISH HAMILTON

Fig. 40. Red printing on title-page, effective because of black printing both above and below the words in colour.

SMALL CAPITALS

Small capitals are useful for display on a title-page as an intermediate in emphasis between capitals and lower case, and are frequently used for the display of matter subsidiary to the title of the book and the name of the author, such as the details of Preface, Introduction, Translation, number of Illustrations and Volumes, Publisher's Address, etc. Small capitals are, in addition, frequently used for displaying an extensive array of honours and degrees held by an author. They are normally set in a line in a small size below his name.

Hansard held the view that in general 'small capitals are used for the purpose of giving a degree more importance to a word or sentence than would be conveyed by printing the same in italic'. He also reminds us that the small capitals, C, O, S, V, W, X and Z, so closely resemble the same letters in the lower case, as to require particular care in the composition to prevent their mixing, as the difference can scarcely be discerned but by their being cast on a thicker body than the others.

COLOUR

The use of colour on a title-page should be concentrated and not dispersed over various displayed items; nor should it be used for individual letters. Red is the most effective colour for emphasis and helps to enliven a mass of type printed in black (Fig. 40). Some printers, notably the late Mr. Bernard Newdigate, whilst agreeing that colour should be massed, made use of the process in reverse, printing a line or two of the title-page in black for outstanding display and printing all subsidiary matter in red. He would print in black what is frequently in red, and vice versa. This has certainly proved pleasing on occasions when there is a sufficient number of displayed lines effectively to sustain the black printing. A witty juxtaposition of black and red, or any other appropriate colour, produces an effect of distinction (Fig. 35).

ORNAMENT

A printer has at his disposal pure typographic ornament in the form of plain rules, swelled rules, flowers, flourishes, and ornamental motifs cast in type metal, as well as vignettes which may be available from either wood-engravings or line-blocks. In addition to the above choice of typographic ornament for a title-page, artists are frequently commissioned by the publisher to design special borders or vignettes for the title-pages of specific publications, particularly when the books are illustrated by the same hand.

If ornament is used it should support and not overpower the type matter by its weight of colour, nor should it on the other hand appear weak. The area occupied by ornamentation should not induce a cramped appearance to the type matter; the type-setting should retain its own just proportions and yet remain easily legible (Fig. 36). Rule work, printers' flowers, and other decorative motifs should not be used merely to 'hold together' a poorly composed page.

All brass rules should be mitred and thus fit perfectly at the corners. Printer's flowers usually have their own special corner pieces; vignettes, including armorial designs and devices, can be attractive but need careful placing. (Fig. 39).

MIXED TYPE FACES

The type face on the title-page is generally that of the text but composed in the various display sizes that are called for. Some of the more skilful printers will introduce, at times, one or more other type faces for emphasis and to impart a degree of decoration. Whilst doing this, it is possible through a judicious choice to retain a visual harmony between the various types, whilst at the same time giving a welcome variety to the page. Indeed, typefounders produce open letters, fully decorative script, and plain titling types for use on title-pages (Fig. 42).

VERSO OF TITLE

The printer's imprint is printed on the verso of the title-page. This page is also used for printing the dates of subsequent new impressions and editions, and the original date of publication if there is no date on the title-page of the first edition. Imposition conforms to that of the title-page (see page 62).

CONTENTS AND LIST OF PLATES

The Contents Page is the next important item in the Prelims. In this early position it enables the reader to ascertain in the easiest manner what a book contains. Preface, Introduction, etc., are often long, and it is as well that the Contents Page should quickly follow the title-page rather than be buried between sections of reading matter. The heading of the Contents Page should be dropped a few lines, like the chapter headings. Contents should be set on a right-hand page, clearly and simply, with the type leaded. In fact, if the type is well leaded there will be no necessity for unsightly leaders connecting the entry with the page reference.

Preliminary items, Appendixes, Glossary, Bibliography, and Index entries on the Contents Page can be set in italic or small capitals to differentiate them from items which refer to the text proper (Fig. 44); but whichever course is chosen, the main typographical emphasis will be applied to the setting of the Contents entries relevant to the main text. Chapter numbers, if shown in roman figures, should not be too conspicuous.

A List of Contents may contain a synopsis of the chapters, in which case the chapter number can be centred conveniently above (Fig. 45). A List of Illustrations, Plates, Maps, or Plans *hors texte* should also be placed on a right-hand page, with the heading ranged with that of the Contents Page. Exception can be made when there are less than, say, six plates or maps, in which case a reference

ROBERT GRAVES

POEMS

1953

CASSELL & COMPANY LTD

LONDON

Fig. 41. Title-page with very few words

FRY'S
ORNAMENTA

OLD FACE
OPEN TITLING

FOURNIER-
LE-JEUNE

BOLD OUTLINE

ORNATA

Fig. 42. Decorative types suitable for display of line or word on a title-page.

Moreau-le-Jeune

𝕭lack 𝕷etter

Fig. 42—*continued*

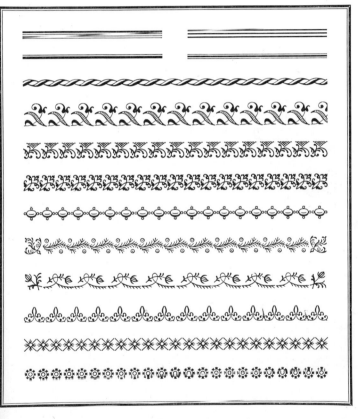

Fig. 43. Borders suitable for use on a title-page

to the illustrations might well be included (if there is space available) as a piece of separate display at the bottom of the Contents Page.

It is not generally necessary to list the illustrations printed in the text; the pagination will show whether a book is complete or not, but with plates *hors texte* there is always a danger of casualties. The List of Plates is, therefore, a guide to what the book should contain.

In a book of two volumes or more, each volume will have its own relevant Contents Page and List of Plates. It is unnecessary to have a Contents Page in a book of fiction when its chapters are merely numbered without chapter titles.

PREFACE AND INTRODUCTION

Both Preface and Introduction open on a recto, with their headings set on the page at the same level as the Contents Page and Chapter Headings. Their head-lines will repeat on the left- and right-hand pages, PREFACE or INTRO-DUCTION respectively, and will not include the title of the book as in the case of the main text. It is often expedient to introduce some moderate typographical difference between introductory pages and the text. This can be most happily achieved by setting these pages in type a size smaller than that used for the text. If the introductory pages are very brief some printers prefer to set them in italic. But whether the Introduction is set differently from the text or not depends very largely on its nature and length and its exact literary relationship to the text.

CONTENTS

Fig. 44. Contents page showing titles of chapters set more prominently than the other items.

CONTENTS

VOLUME I

CHAPTER I

CHAPTER II

CHAPTER III

CHAPTER IV

CHAPTER V

Fig. 45. Contents page with a synopsis for each chapter

6

APPENDIX, AUTHOR'S NOTES, GLOSSARY, BIBLIOGRAPHY AND INDEX

GENERAL

MOST books of any length, exclusive of fiction, children's books, large categories of educational books, Bibles, Prayer Books, and the like, require an Index. Books of a scholarly nature frequently contain, in addition, an Appendix, Glossary, Author's Notes, and a Bibliography. These sections are paginated in arabic numerals continuing on from the text, and we submit that the head-lines on the left-hand and right-hand pages should be the title of the section, e.g. APPENDIX, INDEX, etc. The type for all these subsidiary pages will normally be smaller in size than that of the text.

APPENDIX

The Appendix (plural, Appendixes, except in medical and scientific works, when Appendices should be used) starts on a right-hand page, with the heading ranging with the chapter openings of the text. Where there is more than one Appendix, each will be clearly numbered, and start on a fresh left- or right-hand page.

AUTHOR'S NOTES

It is most important that the typography of Author's Notes should aid the reader to refer back to a reference in the text. The relevant chapter, page number, and actual line on the page should, therefore, be clearly displayed, viz.:

Chapter VIII. Page 99, line 14. *The Advantage of the Woollen Manufacture.* An allusion to the many Acts of Parliament passed in aid of woollen manufactures. The woollen trade of Ireland was destroyed by legislation directed against Irish competition with England.

GLOSSARY

A Glossary has been defined as a 'collection of glosses; list and explanations of abstruse, obsolete, dialectal, or technical terms, partial dictionary'. The setting of the glossary is similar to that of a dictionary in so far as each item can readily be referred to.

BIBLIOGRAPHY

The minimum data for entries of a Bibliography comprise title of book, name of author, date and place of publication, and the name of the publisher. The printer should differentiate clearly between the title of the book and the name of the author by the use of italic, capitals, or small capitals for the former. A more full and elaborate Bibliography of the work of an author requires special typographical treatment of a kind suggested below (Fig. 46). The double vertical rules indicate each separate displayed line or word as printed on the original title-page.

Seven Poems and a Fragment
1922

SEVEN POEMS AND A FRAGMENT || BY WILLIAM BUTLER YEATS || (WOODCUT IN RED) || THE CUALA PRESS || DUNDRUM || MCMXXII

Quarto, size $8\frac{1}{8}'' \times 5\frac{1}{2}''$; pp. xii + 32; price 10s. 6d.

COLLATION: 3 blank leaves; title-page, reverse blank; blank page, on reverse being Table of Contents; blank leaf; text, pp. [1]–24; p. [25] has colophon in red; pp. [26–32] blank.

SIGNATURES: [a] (6 leaves); b to d (3 sheets of 4 leaves); and e (4 leaves). Irish hand-made paper, all edges uncut.

BINDING: dark grey paper boards, light brown linen back, lettered in black on front cover || Seven Poems and a Fragment || By William Butler Yeats || . Grey endpapers to match binding.

The edition consisted of 500 copies.

The Press Mark of the British Museum copy is 011649. i. 108.

Fig. 46. A full bibliographical setting

INDEX

A General Index is placed at the end of a book, but there are, in fact, several other forms of Index, e.g. Index of First Lines for Poetry (Fig. 47), Glossarial Index (Fig. 50), Index to Proper Names, Index to Subjects, etc.

The Index, in whatever form, starts on a recto, and is set in two or more columns unless it is an Index of First Lines. The size of type is generally two sizes smaller than the text. Considerable typographical ingenuity can be exercised in ensuring that the first entry of each alphabetical group is clearly emphasized (Figs. 48–50). The names of books and periodicals should be set in italic, as in the text.

INDEX OF FIRST LINES

A region desolate and wild	*page* 79
A wanderer is man from his birth	195
Affections, Instincts, Principles, and Powers	59
Again I see my bliss at hand	131
And the first grey of morning fill'd the east	198
And you, ye stars	121
Because thou hast believ'd, the wheels of life	59
Before Man parted for this earthly strand	185
Come, dear children, let us away	80
Come to me in my dreams, and then	130
Creep into thy narrow bed	410
Crouch'd on the pavement close by Belgrave Square	396
Down the Savoy valleys sounding	221
Each on his own strict line we move	129
Even in a palace, life may be led well	397
Far, far from here	112

Fig. 47. Index of first lines with white space separating each alphabetical group.

JAMES I, i, 204; ii, 52
Janin, Jules, i, 373
Janus, Frederick, i, 321
Jenkinson, v. Stewart
Jerome, St., ii, 256, 382
Jerome of Prague, i, 147
Jerrold, W., ii, 19
Jewel, Bishop, i, 146
John, King of France, ii, 87
Johnson, Lionel, ii, 17
Johnson, Samuel, i, 44, 68, 69; ii, 14, 116, 117, 356; v. Boswell
Jones, Sir William, i, 262
Jonson, Ben, i, 146, 297; ii, 11
Jowett, Benjamin, i, 260
Julian, Emperor, ii, 146, 379

KENT, Earl of, ii, 303
Kilwardby, R., ii, 43

King, Dr. William, i, 269
Kinglake, A. W., i, 258
Kippis, Andrew, i, 121

LAMB, Charles, i, 57; ii, 12, 17; v. Lamb, 'Letters'
Lami, Giovanni, i, 287
Lang, Andrew, i, 252; ii, 373
Latini, Brunetto, i, 142
Laurinus, Marcus, ii, 29
Lawrence, Col. T. E., v. Thomas
Le Diable Boiteux, ii, 251

MACAULAY, Lord, i, 271, et seq., 303, 318, 356; ii, 176; v. Trevelyan
Machiavelli, i. 96, 205
McKinnon, Mr. Justice, ii, 19
Macnaghten, Sir William, i, 392

Fig. 48. Index with first words of each alphabetical group set in small capitals.

J

James I, i, 204; ii, 52
Janin, Jules, i, 373
Jenkinson, v. Stewart
Jerome, St., ii, 256, 382
Jerome of Prague, i, 147
Jerrold, W., ii, 19
Jewel, Bishop, i, 146
John, King of France, ii, 87
Johnson, Lionel, ii, 17
Johnson, Samuel, i, 44, 68, 69; ii, 14, 116, 117, 356; v. Boswell

K

Kent, Earl of, ii, 303
Kilwardby, R., ii, 43
King, Dr. William, i, 269
Kinglake, A. W., i, 258
Kippis, Andrew, i, 121

L

Lamb, Charles, i, 57; ii, 12, 17; v. Lamb, 'Letters'
Lami, Giovanni, i, 287
Lang, Andrew, i, 252; ii, 373
Latini, Brunetto, i, 142
Laurinus, Marcus, ii, 29
Lawrence, Col. T. E., v. Thomas
Le Diable Boiteux, ii, 251
Le Gallienne, Richard, ii, 397

M

Macaulay, Lord, i, 271 et seq., 303, 318, 356; ii, 176; v. Trevelyan
Machiavelli, i. 96, 205
McKinnon, Mr. Justice, ii, 19
Macnaghten, Sir William, i, 392
Magliabecchi, i, 161, 196, 287, 290, 409; ii, 397

Fig. 49. Index with displayed capital for each alphabetical group. i and ii refer to the volume numbers.

CACOCHES, misprint in F3 for Caroches, carriages, 186

Cadmus, founder of Thebes, changed by Zeus into a serpent, 229

Cæcilius Statius (d. 168 B.C.), Roman comic poet, 224

Cæsar, Madame, a bawd (cf. *Alchemist*, v, 1), compared with Proserpina, queen of the shades, 56

Cæsarian bread, 166, 361

Cæsar's *Commentaries*, C. Edmonds' (*q.v.*) *Observations upon*, 1600–09, 41, 42; his ambition, 265

Cæsar's daughter, Julia, daughter of the emperor Augustus, alleged to be Ovid's Corinna, *q.v.*, 129

Calais, son of Ornytus, a youth admired by Horace's Lydia, 219

Calasiris, a character in the *Aethiopica* of Heliodorus, 260, 367

Caledon, Caledonia, 254

Callimachus (d. *c.* 240 B.C.), grammarian and poet of Alexandria, 333

Calliope, muse of epic poetry, 176

Call, caul, a close-fitting netted cap, 203

Calvin, 337

Camden, William (1551–1623), antiquary, Jonson's master at Westminster School, 6

Canaan, New English, plantation in New England, 272

Canary-wine, 35, 177

Carbonado'd, scored and broiled, 330

Carew, Richard (1555–1620), antiquary, author of *The Survey of Cornwall* (1602), 150

Caroline, dim. of Charles, the infant prince Charles, afterwards Charles II, *q.v.*, 177

Caron, Charon, *q.v.*, 275

Carr, Robert, *see* Somerset, 286

Carract, carat, the measure used in stating the fineness of gold, 188, 200, 271

Cary, Mrs. Anne, e. da. of Sir Edmund Carey, 3rd surviving s. of the 1st lord Hunsdon, mar. before 1608 Sir William Uvedale of Wickham, Hants, *q.v.*, 48

Cary, Sir Lucius, 2nd viscount Falkland (1610–43), soldier and poet; s. of Sir Henry Cary, 178–82

Case, suit of clothes, 257

Cassandra, da. of Priam and Hecuba, foretold the fate of Troy, 129

Cassellius, Cascellius, Aulus (fl. 50 B.C.), Roman jurist, 237

Cassiopea, wife of Cephcus and mother of Andromeda; placed among the Stars, 75

Cast, found guilty, 138

Fig. 50. Page of Glossarial Index

7

ILLUSTRATION

It is not our object in this section to describe the various processes available for reproduction;[1] we merely wish to state a few cardinal points. First, for full-page illustrations, we expect the original to be the finest of which each particular artist is capable, regardless of whether it always 'matches' type or not. Wood-engravings now, as always, can most easily be made to harmonize with pages of type (Fig. 51) and, in more recent times, this applies to an even greater degree to the ordinary line-block whether in colour or in black only. The line-block has been so perfected that brushwork and elaborate pen work can be reproduced, which through excellence of design and contrast to the type often yield a rich result. Such contrast can be further emphasized by Lithography (now undergoing a revival), Etchings, Stencils, and the Collotype process. In any case, the printing of illustrations is a stimulating challenge to the ingenuity of the printer within the economic limits set by the publisher.

Full-page illustrations of any kind are best printed or guarded in as right-hand pages, since these pages lie flat more easily in an opened book and are thereby the easier to contemplate. Single plates should be securely guarded into the book when binding, plates that are merely tipped in come loose in time. Plates that are grouped together at the end of a book require a half-title between the end of the text and the first plate. Illustrations that are interspersed in the type throughout the text demand processes (line-blocks, wood-engravings, or half-tone blocks) that can be printed at the same time as the type unless there are special reasons to the contrary. The captions should be set two sizes smaller than the text type, and each caption should bear a number for ready reference when the illustrations

[1] See *Processes of Graphic Reproduction* by Harold Curwen, 1934.

First Night

Maximilian found the doctor in the hall, just as he was drawing on his black gloves. 'I am in rather a hurry,' the doctor called out to him brusquely; 'Signora Maria hasn't slept all day and has just fallen into a light slumber. I don't have to tell you to avoid any noise which would awaken her, and should she wake, she should not be allowed to speak. She must remain quite quiet without moving —only mental activity is healthy at the moment. Please tell her some more of your phantasies, so that she has to listen quietly.'

Fig. 51. Page with wood-engraving by Imre Reiner harmonizing with type.

And ech of hem tolde oother what hem liste.
 " Cosyn," quod she, " if that I hadde a space,
As I have noon, and namely in this place,
Thanne wolde I telle a legende of my lyf,
What I have suffred sith I was a wyf
With myn housbonde, al be he of youre kyn."
 " Nay," quod this monk, " by God, and Seint Martyn !
He is na mooré cosyn unto me
Than is this lief that hangeth on the tree.
I clepe hym so, by Seint Denys of Fraunce !
To have the mooré cause of áqueyntaunce
Of yow, which I have lovéd specially,
Aboven allé wommen sikerly ;
This swere I yow on my professioun.
Telleth youre grief, lest that he come adoun,
And hasteth yow, and gooth youre wey anon."

Fig. 52. Line-block from a drawing by Brian Robb, illustrating 'The
   Shipman's Tale' from Chaucer's *The Canterbury Tales*.

ILLUSTRATION 83

are of a documentary nature. It is not, however, always necessary to list the cuts that appear in the text in the List of Illustrations in the preliminary pages as in the case of plates *hors texte*.

It is often necessary to insert tissue paper to protect each plate reproduced by the more delicate and vulnerable processes such as collotype, etching, stencil, or copper-engraving. Whilst the caption may be printed on the tissue for quick reference, it is essential that it should also be printed in a more permanent manner, for instance, underneath each plate, as tissues finally become casualties in one way or another in the course of time, either through crumpling or becoming entirely detached from the book.

Where illustrations are grouped together at the end of a book, the half-title page preceding them may be used for printing the order in which the plates appear, with full captions for each item.

It is customary to number plates *hors texte* in roman numerals to avoid confusion with numbered illustrations in the text, and to avoid any possible confusion between the number of the plate and the pagination of the book.

A common form of illustration is to intersperse decoration throughout the book by the use of headpieces and vignettes, in contrast to full-page designs. In such cases the public expects a book at a moderate price, and as it would be uneconomic if the decorative material could not be printed at the same time as the type, wood-engravings or line-blocks are particularly suitable processes for the purpose (Fig. 52).

PAPER, PRESSWORK, BINDING AND JACKETS

PAPER

PAPER is made in infinite variety to meet the needs of every kind of book, and the right choice of paper for the particular book in hand is obviously of great importance. Type faces that are light in 'colour' demand paper that is more absorbent than the harder papers suitable for the heavier type faces. For instance, Baskerville shows itself to greater perfection on a hard smooth paper, while the lighter-faced Caslon needs the support of a softer, more absorbent paper. Few of our types show to advantage on 'art' shiny paper, but of these the sturdy Plantin and Times are the most effective. The most suitable kind of paper for the ordinary unillustrated book is one that is flexible, compact, smooth or fairly smooth, pleasant in smell, touch, and colour—colour just off-white avoids eye-dazzle. Papers that are thick and flabby should be avoided. Book papers are divided into two distinct categories, namely, laid and wove. Laid papers show intersected wire marks across the sheet, whilst a wove paper presents an even, smooth surface. The laid lines on hand-made paper are a natural result of making paper by hand from a laid mould, which preceded the invention of the wove mould by some centuries. Both laid and wove moulds are in use today in the hand-made paper mills. On the other hand a laid machine-made paper is an anomaly, originating in the attempt to acquire the prestige of a hand-made paper. Wove paper yields the finest results for printing on modern power-driven machines, provided the texture and surface are of the best; indeed, the texture of some of the best and heavier wove papers provides a sufficiency of bulk which is undoubtedly an attraction to publishers. This book, for instance, is printed on a wove paper. All papers should be made so that they can be fed into the machine the right way round, i.e. with the fibres running from top to bottom. This helps to prevent the book from cockling when bound.

Hand-made papers, both wove and laid, should be damped before printing, unless they are plate finished, i.e. with a very smooth surface. Deckle edges are naturally produced during the process of making hand-made papers but are entirely artificial in the manufacture of machine-made papers. Deckles collect dirt, particularly on books which are housed in our present-day industrial towns; they are also an inconvenience to the reader in turning over the pages, and even on hand-made papers should be trimmed off. Machine mould-made papers are manu-factured from a mixture of rags and sulphite woodpulp, but unlike hand-made papers they should not be damped, as there would be danger of cockling when dry again, owing to the fact that they are not one hundred per cent rag content.

The choice of paper for books with illustrations in the text is, of necessity, conditioned by the kind of illustration and process of reproduction to be used. The choice of paper for plates *hors texte* is usually different from that chosen for the text paper as almost invariably these plates are printed by processes other than letterpress. An approxi-mate match should be arrived at, however, in the colour of the two papers chosen.

PRESSWORK

An essential feature of presswork is the preparation of the impression cylinder and the regulation of the ink so that a regular, even, and crisp impression is obtained over the whole type area. This even impression should sharply de-fine each letter without blurring or under inking. A good black ink is rich and full in colour in its natural state. A cheap black ink is in the end false economy, and tends to produce a black with an unpleasant brown, green, or blue tinge. The kind of paper used affects the density of ink required: much less ink for instance is needed when print-ing on a hand-made paper that has been damped.

BINDING

In England, among other countries, it is the custom to bind or rather to 'case' books in boards. A well-bound book is easy to open, and this result is largely achieved by good sewing, accurate case-making, proper casing-in, and the use of flexible glue on spine and linings. Endpapers also add considerably to the strength of the casing-in, and assist the mull[1] and tapes to hold the book together. They are also a protection against particles of glue or of damp permeating through to the first pages of type matter, and they give a tidiness to the insides of the boards by concealing tapes, mull, and 'turnover' of the cloth. Endpapers should there- fore be strong and should always be folded and cut with the grain running the right way for the boards; this helps to avoid any cockling of the boards after binding. It is only possible to make certain of these conditions if the end- papers are chosen separately from the text paper. End- papers can also be made effective for a decorative purpose by the application of design or by using patterned or coloured papers.

All bound books should be lettered on the spine with the title and name of the author, so that a book can be instantly identified in its final resting place on the shelves of a library after the jacket has been destroyed or removed. On the other hand, it is unnecessary, except for embellish- ment, to have lettering on the side of the book, particularly when the book is published complete with a jacket, as the jacket will give all the relevant information as long as the volume is in the bookshop.

Gold leaf still remains the clearest and most permanent material for applying the lettering to the cloth. At its sim- plest, a brass block can be cut from a model set up in type adjusted for size and letter-spacing by the brasscutter. It is more satisfactory, however, to have lettering drawn for the

[1] Mull is a bookbinder's muslin stiffened and rather easier to use than cambric. It strengthens the joint of back and boards and sup- plements the holding power of the endpapers.

spine of each individual book. It must be borne in mind that a negative effect, i.e. that of white on black, is produced by the use of gold on a dark cloth, but a positive, i.e. of black on white, if the gold is put on a very light cloth. Such consequences may have little effect on lettering, but can profoundly alter the whole balance of a design or decoration. Allowance must be made for the effect of shading caused by the stamping of the lettering on to binding cloth, which is a yielding material. Though the spine of a book is always a relatively narrow area, it is desirable whenever possible to have the lettering running across (without being too small) rather than running up or down the spine. Drawn lettering can most easily be adapted to economy of space without loss of legibility, and can occasionally be aided by ligatures, e.g.

POOL (type)

POOL (drawn lettering).

An alternative method is to have standard alphabets drawn to serve as models to the brasscutter. For those engaged in handling large numbers of different titles, this method has much to commend it (Fig. 53). The brass-cutter bears much responsibility, for, whether the lettering is specially drawn or a standard model supplied, he must adjust carefully the letter-spacing and scale of the letters. Failing gold leaf, foils are sometimes used for applying the lettering, but a great deal of ink blocking is also done.

The decoration of a bookbinding, at one time an important and often lovely feature, has fallen into neglect especially since book-jackets have played such an important part. Paper-bound books lend themselves, like jackets, to a greater variety of treatment, both graphic and typographic, whereas the means of reproducing designs on cloth are very limited. The paper cover fulfils the double function of jacket and cover, but its life is ephemeral.

D

ABCDE

GHIJKLM

UVWXY

ABCDE

LMNO

Fig. 53. Portions of alphabets designed for use on bindings
(Jonathan Cape)

THE BOOK-JACKET

The last stage of book production is the Book-jacket. Although extraneous to the book as a whole, it demands the most careful and ingenious treatment. Originally the purpose was mainly protective, but in the course of time it has acquired a potent 'sales' value in addition to its function of supplying in miniature poster form relevant information of title, name of author and publisher. Most books are, as a matter of course, displayed for sale in bookshops both in this country and through export abroad. The book-jacket should appeal to prospective buyers at a first impression, and when there are books displayed of a similar kind but issued by different publishers, the excellence of the jacket will play a competitive part.

The approach to designing a book-jacket is more simple in some kinds of books than others. Books on more scholarly and specialized subjects, which do not lend themselves to ordinary methods of salesmanship, can well have jackets in a typographic style tending to harmonize with the typography of the book itself. Again, jackets for a standard library such as *Everyman*, where new titles are added from year to year, must have a recognizable style which will remain inviting over a long period. It is in the more general and highly competitive field that the jacket presents its greatest demand for novelty and difference from its fellows. Great variety can, of course, be achieved by employing different processes for different kinds of designs. Where work has been specially commissioned from artists, lithography, four-colour half-tone work, and the line-block (in colours or black only) may be used for reproduction, the choice of any one of these processes will depend on the nature of the original design. When a photograph is to be reproduced, either a half-tone block, photo offset, or photogravure is necessary.

The most economic and not the least effective is the purely typographic jacket. Typefounders offer a large number of display borders and faces of the requisite weight and carrying power for the setting of jackets (Figs. 54 and 57). By the skilful use of this wealth of material, it should be possible to achieve effects which will at the same time attract the attention of buyers standing some distance from the bookshop window or shelf, and yet be agreeable when the book is actually in the hand. We should not infer that all jackets should be bold in their type-setting; on the contrary, variety is essential, and this can be achieved in many ways by displays ranging from the simple to the ornate, in conjunction with variety in colour of inks and colour of papers. Many publishers produce books with certain similarities of style running through the jacket designs of most of their publications with the object of making their own publications recognizable by the book-buying public.

When publisher and printer are able to work exceptionally closely together, it is possible to assist the display by the kind of wording or 'blurb' supplied. This blurb may at times be an integral part of the typographic design on the front of a jacket, supplementary to the displayed words of title and author. The spine of a jacket, although narrow in relation to the side, should not be neglected; many books are displayed showing their spines only. When the area is sufficient for a continuation of an attractive display, the opportunity should not be neglected.

ORPLID

ALBERTUS

CHISEL

Fig. 54. Display types suitable for jackets

FIGGINS SHADED

ULTRA BODONI

ELONGATED ROMAN

TIMES HEAVY TITLING

ULTRA BODONI CONDENSED

GILL SANS BOLD

SANS SHADOW LINE

CAMEO RULE

PERPETUA BOLD

Fig. 54.—*continued*

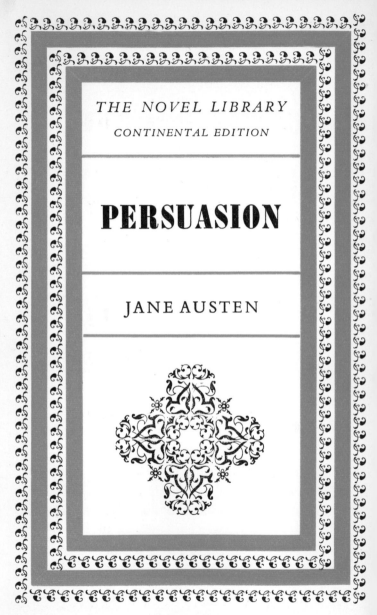

THE NOVEL LIBRARY

CONTINENTAL EDITION

PERSUASION

JANE AUSTEN

Figs. 55 and 56.
Fronts of jackets, making use of coloured ink.

THE

DEEP

BLUE

SEA

A NEW PLAY

BY

TERENCE
RATTIGAN

Fig. 56

Monotype

Typefounders

Fig. 57. Borders suitable for jacket display

9
MISCELLANEOUS

SWASH LETTERS

S WASH capitals are a set of letters supplementary to certain italic capital letters for use at the beginning and sometimes at the end of words in displayed lines. Swash letters are, in fact, in the nature of an exuberant flourish (swell letter), decorative in effect, which had its origin in the scriptorium. Whilst swash capital letters can be used for chapter openings and on the various preliminary pages, and even on rare occasions on headlines, it is on a title-page that they can most fully be brought into play.

Swash capital letters need careful and consequently slow composition, the letters being inserted by hand and meticulously spaced. The kerns are delicate and are inclined to break, and a vigilant watch must be kept throughout all stages of production to avoid broken letters.

Any display incorporating swash letters should be kept within the bounds of reticence; their too frequent use becomes tiresome. Only when they are used in moderation can the element of surprise and fancy be maintained (Fig. 58).

NEW BRUNSWICK

not

NEW BRUNSWICK

The Black Prince (plain)   *The Black Prince* (swash)

Fig. 58. Examples of Caslon swash capital letters in use

Of the fifteen type faces shown on pages 14 and 15, few are supplied with swash letters. Only Caslon italic and Garamond italic are fully equipped in capitals.

SWASH LOWER-CASE ITALIC LETTERS

The principles governing the use of swash lower-case letters are similar to those governing swash capitals, but more frequently they will be used only as terminal letters to displayed words set in capitals and lower-case italic.

BRACKETS AND SWELLED RULES

We have already referred to the primary use of brackets in the section on Rules of Composition (see page 4), but they can be enlisted for other purposes. To some eyes, pages that for various reasons are without head-lines look unduly spartan; this is relieved when the pagination is set within brackets, thereby giving a suggestion of ornamentation. In the setting of plays, the square bracket is available for several minor functions (Figs. 24 and 25), whilst in poetry, when the poems themselves are numbered rather than titled, the setting of the pagination in brackets will clearly make sufficient difference between the two sets of numerals appearing on the same page.

Miss Peggy Lang has drawn attention to the value of the swelled rule as an element of design and as a means of focusing the eye on the vertical centre of the page. She defines the scope of the swelled rule well when she says: 'It signifies hiatus rather than separation or finality. While its weight achieves emphasis, the tapering ends prevent obtrusiveness, and by its own graduation it brings into harmony varying weights of type. It lends shape to the traditional title-page and helps to overcome the bareness normally attending the short modern title. A single rule, or pair, emphasizes and adorns chapter headings, while a shorter dash signifies pause at the ends of sections.'[1]

Swelled rules are supplied by typefounders both in their simple and decorative forms. As with swash letters, their employment can easily become tiresome if over-done, and their use by unskilled hands can bring much ugliness to the printed page. A well-selected decorative swelled rule can impart as much beauty to a page as a vignette or printers' flowers. But when the swelled rule is of the simpler, plain sort, whether used for decoration or for some specific purpose, it should be finely tapered. The ultra-fat sort invariably annoys the reader and rarely justifies itself for use with text or display types used in books.

[1] 'Swelled Rules and Typographical Flourishes', by Peggy Lang. *Signature*, No. 9. 1938.

PRINTERS' FLOWERS, ETC.

Printers' flowers first came into use in the early part of the
sixteenth century and have remained an important typographic medium for decoration to this day. They have an
interesting history[1] and many beautiful designs have sur-
vived through the centuries as a rich heritage at the disposal of book printers. The word 'flowers' is used as a
general term to include decorative motifs cast on type body
as distinct from vignettes and from borders (both plain and
decorative) cast as strips of metal rule.

These flowers are easily obtainable from typefounders
for stock, cost little to buy, and can be quickly assembled;
the printer can choose from the typefounder's catalogue
the design he needs. In this way he avoids the delays and
uncertainties of commissioning an artist to do a special
drawing for the particular book the designs of which would
have to be reproduced by line-block or some other process.
On the other hand, the aesthetic possibilities of flowers are

Fig. 59. Printers' flowers (traditional)

[1] See 'Printers' Flowers and Arabesques', by Francis Meynell
and Stanley Morison. *The Fleuron*, No. 1. 1923.

to a certain extent limited, and there is a danger of tiring
the public through a too-constant repetition of the same
motif, for typefounders' flowers are available to every
printer in the land. This objection would be countered if
more printers were to commission new designs which
would become the possession, through copyright, of their
own particular press. Proprietary type, which was common
enough before the industrial era, is hardly practical today,
but proprietary flowers remain a suitable field for a
printer's initiative. He can thus acquire something different from anything a typefounder can offer, and for a
moderate outlay. It is no easy undertaking to design a
flower complete with corner pieces which can be repeated
in a variety of built-up patterns. It is still more difficult to
produce a design which, satisfactory as a single unit or a
composite motif, shows itself equally effective in a built-up
pattern with other units or motifs, whether the printing is
in black only or in black and colour. Built-up designs of
printers' flowers can be assembled in a great variety of
subtle combinations which can be further enriched by the
use of colour in the printing. In addition to 'flowers' there
is a great variety of ornamental motifs cast in type metal
available to printers for independent use or in combination
with rules and decorative borders (Fig. 60).

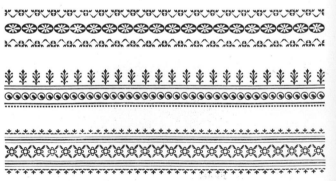

Fig. 60. Composite rule and flower borders

NUMERALS

Roman numerals were used by the earliest fifteenth-century printers because they had no arabic figures. Even today they are sometimes employed, but for special purposes such as the pagination of preliminary pages, for use on chapter headings (see page 36) and for the designation of part numbers, appendixes, etc. They are, too, useful for numbering plates inserted as illustrations *hors texte* (see page 83). Nevertheless they are not quickly interpreted and, while we are all at our ease up to XII through our familiarity with the clock face, the higher numerals require a considerable amount of mental calculation. Those in most frequent use are made up of a combination of the seven capitals I, V, X, L, C, D and M. Any letter, or letters, representing a number of low value which follows a letter of high value must be added to its value and any letter or letters preceding such a number must be subtracted from its value.

1 = I	12 = XII	50 = L	700 = DCC
2 = II	13 = XIII	60 = LX	800 = DCCC
3 = III	14 = XIV	70 = LXX	900 = CM
4 = IV	15 = XV	80 = LXXX	1000 = M
5 = V	16 = XVI	90 = XC	1500 = MD
6 = VI	17 = XVII	100 = C	1700 = MDCC
7 = VII	18 = XVIII	200 = CC	1800 = MDCCC
8 = VIII	19 = XIX	300 = CCC	1895 = MDCCCXCV
9 = IX	20 = XX	400 = CD	1900 = MCM
10 = X	30 = XXX	500 = D	1944 = MCMXLIV
11 = XI	40 = XL	600 = DC	2000 = MM

Arabic numerals do not present any difficulties to the reader, and today their general use is greater than ever in catalogues, bibliographies, for chapter headings, and on title-pages. This has come about through more and more founts of type being issued with both old style and modern arabic numerals in roman and sometimes in italic as well (Fig. 61). This gives to arabic numerals a remarkable degree of flexibility.

1 2 3 4 5 6 7 8 9 0

Modern

1 2 3 4 5 6 7 8 9 0

Old Style

1 2 3 4 5 6 7 8 9 0

Modern Italic

1 2 3 4 5 6 7 8 9 0

Old Style Italic

1 2 3 4 5 6 7 8 9 0

Bold

Fig. 61. Walbaum numerals

Modern numerals range with the capitals of the fount, viz. CHAPTER 25. Old style numerals are less assertive and are designed for use for dates, measurements, etc., in the text and for tabular work. They can also be used ranged with small capitals, viz. CHAPTER 25. Old style numerals are relatively unobtrusive because of the variation of their ranging on the centre of their axis.

1, 2 and 0 range with and are the same size as the lower-case letters a, c, e, etc.

3, 4, 5, 7, and 9 range with and are the same depth as the lower-case letters with descenders g, j, p, q and y.

6 and 8 range with and are the same height as the lower-case letters with ascenders b, d, f, h, k and l, and generally range with capitals as well.

When a fount contains modern and old style numerals, the use of both may be called for in the same book—

modern for the numbering of chapters, old style for numerals in the text, pagination and the dates on the title and verso. These two varieties are particularly useful for bibliographies and catalogues: modern for the item number followed by displayed capitals, the less obtrusive old style for dates and measurements (Fig. 62). The unequal range of old style numerals is most convenient for tabular work where there are solid masses of figures. The eye can pick out each item more easily than would be the case if all numerals presented a solid ranged mass.

For comprehensive instructions as to the proper usage of figures and numerals we refer our readers to *Rules for Compositors and Readers* (Oxford University Press).

22 MARLOW, W., 1740–1813

> Pupil, but not an imitator, of Samuel Scott.
> Painted many views of country seats, bridges,
> etc., both in oil and water-colour
>
> RICHMOND BRIDGE $25\frac{1}{2} \times 36$
> Signed
> *Lent by Colonel M. H. Grant*

23 MORLAND, G., 1763–1804

> Celebrated painter of landscapes with figures
> and animals, coast and fishing scenes, etc.
>
> LANDSCAPE: SANDHILLS WITH FIGURES
> *Lent by Lionel W. Neeld, Esq.*   Panel $16 \times 20\frac{1}{2}$

Fig. 62. Items from a catalogue showing use of modern numerals ranged with the displayed capitals. Old style numerals are used for dates and measurements.

GLOSSARY

Ampersand: The name given to the contraction of 'and', thus: &.

Antiqua: The German name for roman type.

Antique paper: A term used to describe any good book paper with a rough surface.

Art paper: A clay-coated paper, especially suitable for half-tone block printing.

Author's proof: A proof showing corrections made by the author or editor; any departures from MS. after proofing are made at the customer's expense.

Back-up: To print the reverse side of a sheet when one side is already printed, also termed 'perfecting'.

Backs: The back margins of pages, those which adjoin the binding.

Beard: The blank metal sloping away from the actual face of a letter, at its head and foot. Depth of beard varies considerably on different types, and it is often necessary in large sizes to trim the beard in order to obtain closer line spacing.

Binder's brass: A brass block cut especially deep for blocking on cloth bindings.

Black letter: A term loosely covering Old English or Gothic Text.

Bleed: Illustrated books are said to have 'bled edges' when the final trim cuts into the illustrations.

Blind blocking: The blank impression made by a binder's brass block on a cloth binding, i.e. with no ink or foil.

Blocks: A general term which covers line-blocks, half-tones, electros, etc.

Body: The solid shank of the letter. Size of body, i.e. measurement from back to front, is constant throughout any single fount.

Body of the work: The text proper of a volume, as distinct from preliminary pages, indexes and appendixes, etc.

Bold face: A heavy type, frequently used in contrast with types of ordinary weight or colour.

Bolts: The folded edges at the head, tail, and fore-edge of a printed sheet before trimming.

Bowl: Any curved main-stroke of a letter surrounding a closed 'white', or counter.

Calendered paper: Highly glazed paper, so called because the polished finish is given by a stack of cylinders called 'calenders'.

Cancel: A new leaf or leaves reprinted to rectify some error or defect.

Capitals: CAPITALS. Abbreviated to caps. and indicated in manuscript by three underlinings of the words to be thus set.

Captions: Descriptive matter, usually short, placed beneath illustrations. Also known as 'legends'.

Cartridge paper: A hard, tough class of paper made with a rough surface in many grades. Particularly useful for drawing.

Case: In hand composition, a shallow wooden or metal tray, divided into compartments to hold type. In binding, a case is the made-up cover, ready for affixing to the trimmed book.

Cast-off: The preliminary measurement of a manuscript to form an estimate of the number of pages required of a given size of type and area.

Catchline: A temporary descriptive headline on proofs. Also the name given to a short line of type in between two large displayed lines.

Chase: A metal frame, made of wrought iron or steel, into which type is locked, ready for printing.

Clean proof: A proof absolutely correct according to the 'copy' or manuscript.

Cockling: In paper, cockling, a bumpy and uneven condition, may be caused by exposure to damp or uneven heat. Bindings sometimes cockle, i.e. curl out of shape, because the paper used to line the boards has been cut wrongly so that the fibres run across instead of up and down.

Collating: Gathering the various printed sections of a work in the correct sequence.

Collotype: A photo-mechanical non-screen process in which printing is done from a gelatine film, slightly below surface.

Colophon: An inscription at the end of a book often including the printer's imprint and a note of details of production.

Condensed face: Thin, elongated type, useful for long words which are to be displayed in a narrow space.

Contents page: A page included in the preliminary pages of a book giving a list of contents and occasionally a list of illustrations.

Copy: Any matter to be set in type.

Cropping: Work that has been cut down too much is said to have been 'cropped'.

Crown: A standard size of printing paper measuring 15" × 20". A sheet 20" × 30" is known as Double Crown, while Crown Folio, Crown Quarto (Cr. 4to) and Crown Octavo (Cr. 8vo) are half size, quarter size and one-eighth of Crown respectively.

Cursive: The German name Kursiv, for italic types.

Cut: A trade term (American) for illustrations of any kind in the text.

Day (Ben) mediums: 'Mechanical' tints. These are standard designs used on line-blocks to give degrees of tone and texture.

Deckle: The name given to the uneven, rough edges of hand-made paper.

Demy: A standard size of printing paper measuring 17½" × 22½".

Didot point system: Standard of typographical measurement in use throughout Europe; 12 points equal 4·511 mm. and 67·566 points equal 1 inch.

Display work: A term applied to the setting of short lines in varying faces and sizes of type, as distinct from a solid block of type. Advertisements, titles, and headings are 'display' work.

Distribution of type: The operation of returning type to cases after printing, when the type need no longer be kept standing. This is known as 'dis.'.

Double-spread: Two facing pages containing matter which is continuous across both pages.

Drawn-on covers: A form of binding square-backed magazines and books in paper covers. The cover is attached by gluing to the back of the book.

Dropped heads: A name given to chapter headings which are driven down from the top of the page.

Dummy: A sample copy of the proposed work made up before printing with the actual materials, i.e. paper and covers, and cut to the correct size to show bulk, style of binding.

Electrotype: A printing plate made by electrolytically depositing copper on to a mould of wax or lead taken from an original plate or from type, and backed with a lead alloy.

Em: The square of any size of type. Also the name given to the printer's general measure, 12 points, or one-sixth of an inch. This 12-pt. em is the standard for measuring the depth and width of a page.

En: Half an em in any size of type. It is the average width of the letters in a fount and is a useful basis for calculation.

Endpapers: The leaves at the beginning and end of a book, the first and last of which are pasted on to the binding. Endpapers are often decorated, or are sometimes of another colour.

Face of a type: The printing surface of any letter.

First proof: The first pull of a setting after composing which is read from 'copy', after which it is corrected and reproofed as a 'clean' proof.

Flong: Sheets of prepared papier mâché used for making moulds, or matrices, in stereotyping.

Flowers: Decorative motifs cast in metal to type sizes which may be made up into ornaments or borders.

Folio: This term when following a paper size signifies half a sheet of that size. A page number is often referred to as a folio.

Foolscap: A standard size of printing paper measuring $13\frac{3}{8}'' \times 17''$.

Footnotes: Notes at the foot of the page, but still contained within the type area, and set in a size two points smaller than the text size. A line of white usually separates the text from the footnote.

Fore-edge: The edge of a book opposite the binding, i.e. the front edge, as distinct from head and tail.

Format: A covering term for the size and shape of a book.

Forme: The combination of chase, furniture, and type locked up for machine, i.e. the pages imposed in a chase.

Fount: A complete set of any particular type comprising letters, figures, punctuation marks, etc.

Frame: A rack containing type cases at which the compositor works.

French-fold: A sheet of paper with four pages printed on one side only and folded into four without cutting the head. The inside of the sheet is therefore completely blank.

Frontispiece: The illustration facing the title-page of a book.

Full point: A printer's term for a full stop.

Furniture: Wood or metal used to fill in the blank spaces in a forme around and between the pages of type, all held together in the chase.

Galley: A metal tray in which type is placed when composed, before making up into pages. 'Galley-proofs' are proofs pulled from the type contained in these galleys.

Gathering: Placing the sections of a book in their correct order before binding.

Grotesque: The name given to the earliest sans-serif types.

Guarded in: A term used to describe plates which are inserted into a book without being pasted in the ordinary way. The paper area of the plate is wider than the book page, and the projecting part is wrapped round the back of the section.

Gutter: This is an imposition term and applies to the space comprising the fore-edges of pages, plus the trim, where these fore-edges fall internally in the forme.

Hair spaces: Very thin inter-letter and inter-word spaces, equal to $\frac{1}{12}$ of the body width in the middle ranges of a fount series, but varying for very small and larger sizes, thus in 6 pt. the hair space is $\frac{1}{2}$ pt.; in 12 pt. it is $1\frac{1}{2}$ pts.; in 18 pt. it is 2 pts.; and in 24 pt. it is 3 pts.

Half bound: A style of binding having the back and corners covered in a different material from that which covers the sides.

Half-tone block: A printing plate of copper or zinc, photographically produced with the aid of a mechanically ruled screen which reduces the image to a series of dots varying in density according to the tone values of the original.

Hand-made paper: Very durable paper made in individual sheets, by a moulding tray being dipped into a pulp composed of linen rag fibres.

Imposing surface: Known as the 'stone'. A flat surface, usually of metal, on which pages of type are imposed and locked up in chase for printing.

Imposition: The laying-down of pages in position for printing in such a way as to ensure correct sequence when printed and folded.

Imprint: This is the few lines appearing in printed works, which give the name and address of the printer. It is required by an Act of Parliament.

Indent: To begin a line with a blank space, thus setting the line back a little, for instance, the first line of a new paragraph is usually indented.

India paper: A very thin, strong, opaque paper made of rag, used for Bible printing and such other works as require a great many pages in a small bulk.

Initial letters: Large capital letters, often decorative, frequently used at the beginning of a work and sometimes at the beginning of each chapter.

Inner forme: The pages of type which fall on the inside of a sheet: this is the reverse of the 'outer' forme.

Inset: A sheet or part of a sheet placed inside another sheet after folding in order to complete the sequence of pagination for that section. A loose sheet placed inside a book or booklet is also known as an inset.

Italic: A style of type introduced by Aldus Manutius of Venice in which the letters slope to the right as the side heads in this Glossary. Used for emphasis and distinction and indicated by single underlining.

Justification: The name given to the equal and exact spacing of words and letters to a given measure. This is done in mechanical setting as well as by hand.

Kern: This is any part of the face of a letter which extends over the edge of the body and rests on the shoulder of the adjacent letter.

Key: The block or forme in letterpress printing, and the plate or stone in lithography, which acts as guide for position and registration of the other colours.

Laid paper: Paper which shows parallel wire marks, 'laid lines', due to its manufacture on a mould in which the wires are laid side by side.

Lay edges: The edges of a sheet of paper which are laid against the front and side lay gauges of a printing or folding machine. The front lay edge is the 'gripper edge'.

Lay-out: The preparation of copy for setting, with an indication of the type to be used, the type area and the position of blocks, etc., on the page.

Leads: Strips of lead, less than type high, used for spacing out lines of type. They are made to given point thicknesses as follows: 1 pt., 1½ pt. or thin lead, 2 pt. or middle, 3 pt. or thick lead.

Leaf: A 'sheet' of a book which is printed both sides and is equal to two pages.

Leaders: Rows of dots used to guide the eye across the page, often used in tabular work.

Letterpress: Printing from raised type or blocks, as distinct from lithographic, or plate printing.

Letter-spacing: Spacing placed between the letters of a word.

Ligatures: Tied letters, such as fi, ff, fl, etc., cast on one body, to avoid unsightly juxtaposition of fi, ff, fl, etc., and to lessen the risk of damage to kerned letters. Ligatures derive from the early days of printing when letters were cut to resemble formal handwriting.

Line-block: A printing plate of zinc, or occasionally copper, produced photographically and chemically, from which may be printed a reproduction of any line ('black and white') drawing.

Linotype: A composing machine of American origin which sets matter in solid lines or 'slugs'. Generally used in newspaper work.

Literals: Errors made by the printer in setting type from MS.

Lithography: Printing from a porous stone or zinc plate. A planographic process.

Lower case: Letters which are not capitals, thus: a, b, c; also the name given to the case which holds these letters.

Make-ready: The detailed preparation before printing a forme. It includes underlaying and overlaying to overcome inequalities in type and to ensure an impression of proper strength on every part of the printing area.

Make-up: To take type from the galley and arrange in pages to a given depth. In book and magazine work, 'make-up' is the instructions given to the printer for the arrangement of matter and illustrations on each page.

Margins: The white space surrounding a page of printed type.

Marginal notes: Annotations appearing in the side margins of a page. Also called 'side-notes' or 'hanging shoulder notes'.

Matrix: A copper mould into which the image has been struck by a punch, used for casting type. A matrix exists for each character in each fount of type. A papier-mâché mould used in stereotyping is also called a matrix.

Measure: This is the width to which type is set and it is always a stated number of 12-pt. ems.

Medium: A standard size of paper measuring 18″ × 23″.

M.F.: Machine Finished. Describes the surface (varying according to requirements) put upon paper while actually in the machine.

M.G.: Machine Glazed. A class of papers rough on one side and glazed on the other. Used for posters, wrappings, etc.

Modern: A general descriptive term for those type faces which show a characteristic vertical emphasis and fine, bracketed hair-serifs.

Monotype: A composing machine of American origin which casts single types. Generally used in bookwork.

Mould-made paper: A machine-made substitute for hand-made paper.

Nick: A groove appearing in the shank of every piece of type which acts as a guide to the compositor in setting the type the right way up.

Nonpareil: A 6-pt. unit of measurement. The term derives from the name given to a type of 6 pts. in size.

Octavo: The size of a sheet of paper when folded into eight. Abbreviated to 8vo.

Offcut: When a work is printed in an odd size, i.e. not conforming to standard paper sizes, there is very often a surplus piece on the printing paper which is trimmed off. This is known as an offcut.

Offset printing: A process of printing in which the image is transferred from a lithographic stone or plate to a rubber roller which is pressed on to the printing paper.

Old Face: Those type faces characterized by oblique emphasis, lightness of colour, comparatively small differences between the thick and thin strokes, and fairly substantial bracketed serifs, of which the first complete series was cut in France, *c.* 1535.

Opening: Two facing pages of a book.

Overlays: These are used in 'making ready' an illustration and consist of several sheets of paper cut away in such a manner as to give light and shade to the design by altering pressure on the block. There are also mechanical overlays, made by an etching process.

Over-run: To turn over words from one line to the next for several successive lines after an insertion or a deletion.

Outer forme: Pages of type falling on the outside of a sheet.

Page: One side of a leaf. Abbreviated to p. or pp.

Pagination: The numbering of a book on each page.

Perfecting machine: A machine which has two impression cylinders and prints both sides of a sheet at one operation.

Pica: A measurement approximately $\frac{1}{6}$ of an inch. While formerly 'pica' referred to a variable size of type, it is often, though incorrectly, used to denote the 12-pt. em.

Photogravure: A mechanical intaglio process superseding the hand-engraved copperplate.

Plate: An electro or stereo. Also the name given to an insetted illustration in a book.

Point System: The point is the standard of typographical measurement in use today in England and America, and 72 points measure 0·9962″, approximately 1″. Every body size, therefore, is an exact multiple or sub-multiple of every other body size.

Preliminary pages: Those pages of a book containing the matter preceding the main body of the text, such as the half-title, contents page, introduction, etc.

Press proofs: The final proofs of any work before printing.

Proof: A trial print from type or plates.

Proof-reading: This consists of checking the set-up matter from the author's manuscript, and marking the necessary corrections to make the proof correct and tally with the MS. The proof is also marked to conform with the house style of the printer.

Pull: Another name for a proof.

Quadrats: Spaces. Pieces of blank metal less than type height used to fill up spaces and short lines in a page of type. Six sizes are supplied with every fount of type, and in width they are all fractions of the em.

Quarter bound: A style of binding in which the back is of different material from the sides.

Quarto: A size obtained when a sheet is folded into four. Abbreviated to 4to.

Quire: Twenty-four sheets of paper.

Ream: A term denoting a number of sheets of paper ranging from 480 to 516.

Recto: Any right-hand page of a book, that is, odd-numbered.

Register: The exact adjustment of pages back-to-back in printing the second side of a sheet, so that, in folding, the margins will all be correct. In printing work with two or more colours, the positioning of one colour in its correct relation with the rest is known as 'register'.

Retree: A term used to denote defective sheets of paper.

Rivers: Unsightly streaks of white space which appear in pages of printing, caused by over-spacing and by spaces appearing immediately above and below one another.

Royal: A standard size of printing paper measuring $20'' \times 25''$.

Rules: Type-high strips of metal of various widths cut to standard lengths. These are used to print straight lines. Some thicker rules have engraved surfaces which print in a design, and some are cut to show a wavy line surface. Many are obtainable in brass, type-metal, and zinc.

Run: The number of copies required from each forme.

Running head-line: The heading to a page.

Run on: A sentence continued in the same line as the previous one, not a distinct paragraph. Chapters which do not start on a fresh page are said to 'run on'.

Sans serif: A class of types which is characterized by the absence of serifs and the construction of the letters from strokes of equal thickness.

Script: A term applied to any face cut to resemble hand-writing.

Serifs: The finishing strokes at the top and bottom of a letter.

Set: This is the amount of lateral spacing between letters and depends on the thickness of body apportioned to each character. Thus types are spoken of as having 'wide' set or 'narrow' set.

Set-off: The impression made on successive sheets of paper by the wet ink taken from one another, which can be avoided by inter-leaving the printed sheets with blank sheets of paper.

Setting type: This is a recognized term for composing type.

Shank: Sometimes called the stem. It is the exactly rectangular main body of the type.

Signature: In bookwork, the first page of each section bears a distinguishing letter or figure called a 'signature' which proceeds in order throughout the sections of a book, and thus acts as a guide in gathering.

Small capitals: Book founts contain a series of 'small capitals' in most sizes which are smaller than full capitals. SMALL CAPITALS, FULL CAPITALS. They are indicated by double underlinings.

Sorts: Each individual type character is known as a 'sort'.

Special sorts: These are types which are not usually included in a fount and are supplied on request, such as fractions, musical signs, superior and inferior letters and figures.

Standing type: Type which has been printed and is kept in store in readiness for reprinting.

Stereotype: A replica from type or a block, cast in metal from a papier-mâché mould.

Superior letters or figures: Small letters and figures cast on the shoulder of the type so that they print above the level of such letters as s or p, thus: s^a, p^1. *Inferior* letters and figures are also obtainable, and these print below the main part of the letter, thus: a_a, b_1.

Swash letters: Old face italic types with decorative flourishes.

Swelled rules: A class of ornamental rule thick in the centre and graduating down to fine lines at each end.

Tint blocks: Blocks or surfaces used for printing flat background colours.

Tipping in: An illustration or other loose plate, cut to the size of the book, is said to be tipped in when it is pasted at its back margin to the page following.

Titling: Founts of capitals cast so as to occupy the whole of the body size of the type, leaving no beard at the foot.

Type area: The specified amount of space on a page to be filled with type.

Type height: All types are cast to a standard height which is 0·918″ in England. Blocks are mounted to the same height, so that the 'height-to-paper' is uniform in a forme which contains both type and illustration blocks.

Upper case: The top one of a pair of type cases which contains the capital and small capital letters. Also the part of the fount containing the capitals and small capitals.

Verso: The reverse or back of a leaf. All the left-hand, even-numbered pages of a book.

Watermark: A design introduced into sheets of paper during manufacture made by wire worked into the desired shape It serves chiefly as a trade mark.

Whole bound: A volume bound entirely in one material.

Work and turn: A method of imposing work in which the matter is printed on both sides of the sheet in such a way as to yield two complete copies after cutting.

Wove: A term applied to papers made on an ordinary web in which the wires are woven, used in contradistinction to *laid.*

Wrong fount: An error in composing caused by sorts of one fount becoming mixed with another and appearing in the matter set.

HAND-LIST OF BOOKS

Unless otherwise stated the books listed have been published in London.

In the Day's Work, by Daniel Berkeley Updike. Humphrey Milford. 1924.

Four Centuries of Fine Printing, by Stanley Morison. Benn. 1924.

The Printer, His Customers and His Men, by John Johnson. Dent. 1933.

The Printing of Books, by Holbrook Jackson (second edition). Cassell. 1947.

The Typographic Arts, by Stanley Morison. The Sylvan Press. 1949.

First Principles of Typography, by Stanley Morison. Cambridge Authors' and Printers' Guide Series. Cambridge University Press. 1951.

Designing Books, by Jan Tschichold. New York: Wittenborn Schultz Inc. 1951.

The Illustration of Books, by David Bland. Faber & Faber. 1951.

The Making of Books, by Seán Jennett. Faber & Faber. 1951.

Nineteenth-Century Ornamented Types and Title Pages, by Nicolette Gray. Faber & Faber. 1951.

A History of the Old English Letter Foundries, by T. B. Reed, edited by A. F. Johnson. Faber & Faber. 1952.

The Work of Jan van Krimpen, by John Dreyfus. The Sylvan Press. 1952.

Printing Types, Their History, Forms and Use, by Daniel Berkeley Updike (third edition). Oxford University Press. 1952.

Meisterbuch der Schrift, by Jan Tschichold. Ravensburg: Otto Maier Verlag. 1952.

SUBJECT INDEX

NOTE. Neither the contents of the Glossary nor the Hand-list of Books is included in the Index.